Principles of
Lutheran Theology

CARL E. BRAATEN

Principles of
Lutheran Theology

D0068163

FORTRESS PRESS   PHILADELPHIA

Chapter 6, "The Christocentric Principle," is an abridgment of the author's essay in *Interpretation* 25 (October 1971): 480–99, entitled "The Significance of Apocalypticism for Systematic Theology," and is used here by permission.

Biblical quotations, unless otherwise noted, are from the Revised Standard Version of the Bible, copyright 1946, 1952, © 1971, 1973 by the Division of Christian Education of the National Council of the Churches of Christ in the U.S.A. and are used by permission.

Library of Congress Cataloging in Publication Data

Braaten, Carl E., 1929-
   Principles of Lutheran theology.

   Bibliography: p.
   Includes index.
   1. Theology, Lutheran. 2. Theology, Doctrinal.
3. Lutheran Church—Doctrinal and controversial
works. I. Title.
BX8065.2.B67 1983   230'.41'018   82-16542
ISBN 0-8006-1689-8

9754I82 Printed in the United States of America 1-1689

To My Mother
CLARA AGNES BRAATEN

Contents

Introduction

This book deals with the specifically confessional criteria of Christian theology operative in the Lutheran tradition. The setting of this kind of reflection is properly the church and the seminary, not the secular university and a department of religious studies in general. The decision whether this fact of location diminishes or augments its appeal as a piece of theology will depend on the expectations of the readers. One thing is clear: for good or bad this confessional mode of reflection is being done today only in the context of the church and its theological schools. The university has opted for the scientific study of religious phenomena, surrendering the claim to truth in a normative sense. For this reason the discipline of theology as such has virtually vanished from the secular university. There may be a few exceptions where theology is still done as an academic discipline in the modern university, but most of this falls into the category of philosophical or fundamental theology, not confessional or dogmatic theology.

Christian theology is always a human attempt to understand the Christian faith in light of our knowledge of its historical origins and the challenges of the contemporary period. The search for this knowledge has become more and more difficult with the increase of specialization and the sheer quantification of objective data. When theology is divided into so many fields of specialization, it is possible to get immersed in some of the parts and miss the sense of the whole. The student finds it tempting to study all about the Bible without discovering what the Bible is all about. No wonder we hear so much curricular jargon about interdisciplinary teaching and integration, of "getting it all together."

Integration does not happen by adding up the sum of the parts. It is possible to work one's way through an academically rigorous curriculum of a sophisticated theological school, acquiring much knowledge about the Bible, church history, contemporary theology, and ministerial skills, and still not be able to make a single theological statement, let alone preach the gospel with insight and passion. What is missing? Integration cannot happen, we have said, by using the additive method. It is organically linked to the factor of identity. Theology, however, is undergoing a kind of identity crisis. It is wandering in the wilderness of endless methodological prolegomena, searching for the way to the promised land of meaning and truth. Theology is once again putting the question of its own identity. Unsure of where this is rooted, theology has recently played the game of "relevance roulette." But there is no way of being relevant without a secure sense of identity. Theology must go back to basics, and this means back to its origins in the gospel itself.

The search for Christian identity and its articulation in contemporary terms has given rise to a smorgasbord of theological schools. Pluralism, like specialization, is one of the telling features of present-day theology. Among Lutherans alone we have almost every kind of modern label: Erlangen, Lundensian, eschatological, process, existentialist, hermeneutical, language analysis, secular, liberation, feminist, and what not. These labels are sure signs that Lutherans, like all others, must work to pour the good wine of the gospel into new wineskins. We cannot merely restate the ancient traditions of the gospel; we must be involved in an ongoing revision of our understanding of the Christian message. The old *content* of faith—the same yesterday, today, and forevermore—is always received under the conditions of a new *context* of life; both content and context are taken up into the process of theological reflection.

Conservatives are usually protective of content, fearing that liberals are giving away too much to context. Conservatives may choose to ignore the contextual factor, but they cannot escape it. The best way to prevent the reduction of the gospel to context is to become aware of one's own presuppositions. Words like "situation," "context," "horizon," "*Sitz im Leben,*" "frame of reference," "paradigm," "model," and the like are all indications that contemporary theologians are trying to thematize the contextual factor in the process of interpretation and thereby increase the chance of grasping the content of faith in a disciplined way.

It is clear that many factors must work together in the doing of theology. First of all, there is the existential factor of faith itself. This is the starting point of real theology. St. Anselm defined theology as "faith in search of understanding." Luther spoke of a "theology of the heart" (*theologia pectoralis*). Kierkegaard stressed the quality of infinite personal passionate interest in religious reflection. Tillich defined faith as ultimate concern and Bultmann as existential commitment. This particular factor of personal faith-stance is more conspicuously at work in this book than in any others I have written. It is the "here I stand" manifesto of my career as a theologian.

The second factor that is brought into play in doing theology is that of the Christian tradition. We cannot swallow the tradition whole. There is a lot of rotten stuff in the history of Christianity. The task is to discover the norms in, with, and under the traditions by which to criticize them. I have drawn upon the Lutheran tradition as a resource of criticism in the service of the gospel—which is what makes Christianity authentically Christian in every age. If another tradition would serve us better to critique Christianity by the claim of the gospel, we would be instantly on its side. It is not our intention to push the Lutheran tradition for its own sake. When Lutheranism achieves its goal of reforming the church, it goes out of business as a confessional movement. Otherwise it lingers on as a sect. And that is a fate we would wish to avoid at all costs.

A third factor we have already mentioned—the contextual factor. It is not nearly as prominent in this book as in my other writings. Yet the contemporary horizon is implicit in the process of retrieving insights from the tradition to make sense of the gospel today. My partisan interest can hardly be missed in the following chapters. I wish to revise not only the Christian tradition in general, but also the Lutheran articulation of the gospel in particular, from the standpoint of the contemporary rediscovery of the eschatological horizon of primitive Christianity. My belief is that this is also most engagingly effective in the communication of the gospel to the contemporary world. I belong to a particular school of thought—the eschatological school—but the days when this could be thought fashionable are past. I am aware of the danger of modernism, of playing around with passing fads. Some critics have dismissed the so-called "theology of hope" as one of the fads, along with the theology of the "death of God," theology of play, ecotheology, and the like. I do not regard the eschatological motif of Christian faith as the stuff of which fads are made. A theology that pivots on the hope engendered by the message of Easter, that Jesus lives, is hardly a fad. It is basic Christianity.

Fourth, there is the constructive factor of theology. Every generation of theologians is doing a new thing in conformity to criteria of adequacy and rationality. The alternative is fideism and obscurantism. Our aim is to make new theological statements that make sense under the modern conditions of experience and knowledge. Theology should be reasonable but not rationalistic. Christianity is a christocentric religion of faith, hope, and love. It would be unreasonable to speak of it otherwise. What is the reason of this faith, of this hope? We are asking about the logic of

the matter, of our thought and speech about God and his saving revelation in Jesus Christ. How can we verify or falsify a theological statement
that purports to be meaningful and true? If there be no way, then we fall
victim to a pointless relativism. This constructive factor is particularly
strong in apologetics and systematics. It is less pronounced, though not
absent, in a study such as this one which calls upon specifically confessional criteria that make sense within the fellowship of a particular family
tradition.

Finally, there is the practical factor. We do not do theology for
theology's sake, but solely for the sake of communicating the message of
the gospel, for the mission of the church, and for helping the laity to
engage the modern world. The theology we do intends to mesh gears
with what pastoral leaders and their congregations do in church, namely,
in preaching, worship, and caring for each other, and also what they do
in the world, relating to their struggles for peace and justice, their daily
work in the world, their family and social life.

In this book I have lifted up seven principles of Lutheran theology that
can help students of theology, pastoral leaders, and the Christian laity to
interpret the gospel rightly in an orthodox manner. Orthodoxy means
"straight teaching" about the Christian faith. It is not an achievement of
which we can boast; it is the aim of serious theological inquiry. Why
would a theologian opt for another intention? The formative principles
of our Lutheran confessional tradition aim to instruct us in our ongoing
inquiry into the language of the gospel and the meaning of faith in
Christ. They direct us to what the Scriptures say, the claim of the gospel,
and the essentials of the Christian faith.

A few words in explanation of the genre of this book might be useful.
The work as a whole is a product of many years of wrestling with issues
of Lutheran identity under the broad rubric of a hermeneutics of the
gospel. This is the only specifically Lutheran book I have ever attempted
to write. The word "Lutheran" has scarcely ever been used in my other
publications. Nevertheless, the confessional criteria have been implicitly
operative all along, as many a foe and friendly critic have detected
behind the lines. Every theologian who aims to present simply the Christian faith as such carries a certain load of traditional baggage; some
elements of the tradition may get in the way, other parts may be
generative of insight. I believe that the confessional criteria addressed in
this book have served in both respects and account for the best and the
worst in the Lutheran tradition. But I do not believe the baggage should
be thrown overboard. A more responsible approach is to interpret the

classical criteria of confessional theology under the impact of a contemporary theory of hermeneutics and how it works to retrieve the symbols of the Christian faith.

I have been teaching and writing various portions of this book over the past twenty years for seminary classes, pastoral conferences, lay institutes of theology, faculty colloquies, theological societies, and what not. This accounts for the variety of style and level of rhetoric. To my knowledge no theologian has ever boiled the Lutheran tradition down to seven principles of interpretation. There is more than one way to slice the pie of tradition, and I do not claim to have discovered the best possible way. Nevertheless, these principles have been for me the most useful handles on a very rich and complex heritage of church life and doctrine. I have never been able merely to repristinate the doctrines of the Lutheran church in the form of a theology of its confessional writings, as though getting it all down right could serve directly as the dogmatic or systematic theology the church needs today. I am committed to a revisionist model of doing theology, as every new generation must contribute its own gift to the ongoing task of interpreting the gospel under ever new conditions of historical experience.

The first of the seven principles we call "The Canonical Principle." Here we aim to explain the basis and meaning of the authority of Scripture *(sola scriptura)* in continuity with Luther's Christ-and-gospel-centered "canon within the canon" *(was Christum treibt)*. The second is 'The Confessional Principle," which derives the binding character of the confessional writings of the Lutheran Reformation from their hermeneutical function to ground Christian identity in the gospel of free justifying grace, received through faith alone, and solely for Christ's sake *(sola gratia, sola fide, propter Christum).* In the third chapter on "The Ecumenical Principle" we argue that in the quest for Christian unity today it continues to be enough *(satis est)* to agree concerning the Word and Sacraments, and that demands extraneous to the gospel should not be imposed as requirements for a reunion of the divided churches.

"The Christocentric Principle" forms the central thrust of a theology deeply indebted to Luther's evangelical reform of the catholic church. The burden of this principle today is to clarify what sense it makes to preach Jesus Christ as the hope of the world's salvation and what nonsense to relativize the exclusive claim of the gospel in an age so conscious of religious pluralism. In "The Sacramental Principle" we are giving a theological account of the kind of sacramental realism that finds the embodiment of the gospel *in, with,* and *under* the earthly elements of water, bread, and wine—treasure in earthen vessels. The intent of this chapter is not to develop a theology of the Christian sacraments *in toto*, but to illustrate through a discussion of the Lord's Supper the meaning of the old Lutheran incarnational axiom: the finite is capable of the infinite *(finitum capax infiniti)*.

Homiletics in the Lutheran tradition has been governed by the law/gospel distinction. In the chapter on "The Law/Gospel Principle" we bemoan the loss of this distinction in contemporary theories of preaching and sermon design, since it has given way to autobiographical storytelling, psychologizing speculation, and sociological harangue. Preaching can hardly scale the heights of gospel when the backbone of law has been broken. A parallel distinction is commonly referred to as "The Two-Kingdoms Principle," which frames a Christian doctrine of God and the world, hinging on two contrasting ways in which God is at work. This distinction is grounded in Luther's doctrine of the distinction between the hidden God *(Deus absconditus)* and the revealed God *(Deus revelatus)*.

The treatment of all these classical elements of Lutheran confessional theology provides a contemporary interpretation of the old scholastic principle: to distinguish without separation in order to unite without confusion. Lutheranism has often been charged with dualistic distortions and dichotomous separations. The hermeneutical key to making proper distinctions without separation lies in the recovery of the full eschatological concept of God and his kingdom. The eschatological core of Jesus' message is the point of departure for a historical account of the origins of Christology in the apostolic witness, and the kingdom of God becomes the spinal concept of a systematic theology oriented to the gospel of the church and its mission in world history. It is this eschatological factor that offers the promise of renewal for the church and a revision of theology. Thus, the application of the eschatological perspective to an interpretation of the confessional criteria in theological method continues the more comprehensive project of theology carried on in all my previous publications, most notably *The Future of God* and *The Flaming Center*.

Lutheran School of Theology at Chicago   CARL E. BRAATEN
June 1982

1 The Canonical Principle

THE CANON

The Bible was the chief document of the Reformation. To understand the Reformation and the life of the churches it created, it is necessary to study Martin Luther's encounter with the Bible. Luther's struggle to find a gracious God was always accompanied by his interpretation of Scripture. His call for the church to reform itself arose out of the gospel he discovered through biblical exegesis. Luther was professor of Bible at the University of Wittenberg. He produced no systematic theology like Melanchthon or Calvin. His theology was worked out through exegetical lectures and expository preaching on the Old and New Testaments. For Luther theology and preaching were forms of biblical exposition. He possessed a radical confidence in the Word of Scripture on account of its gospel message.

The popular view of Luther rediscovering the Bible—or emancipating the Scriptures—is a misconception. There were many Bibles in Germany before Luther's time. His own Augustinian order encouraged a devout study of Holy Scripture. There were thousands of copies of the Latin Bible (Jerome's translation) to be found in churches, schools, and monasteries. There were also various translations into German in Luther's day. Humanistic scholars, like Reuchlin and Erasmus, were producing critical texts of the Bible in Hebrew and Greek so that when Luther began to study the Bible in earnest, he had access to the Bible in its original languages.

Luther's unique contribution was to produce a translation of the Bible into the language of the common people, peasants, and merchants. The invention of printing made it possible to bring this popular version to the masses so that the Reformation could be carried forward with a laity that knew the Scriptures. To advance the teachings of the Reformation, Luther provided prefaces for almost all of the books. Some of his sharpest and most memorable critical judgments on Scripture are to be found in these prefaces. Luther said, for example, that he did not wish to have books like James and Revelation in the Bible. Books that really belong in the canon of Scripture are only those that clearly communicate the gospel. Books that fail to communicate the gospel clearly must hold a lower rank in the canon.

Luther did not produce a new canon. He operated with the canon that had been in actual use in the church. However, he made fundamental distinctions between the books of the Bible by applying a christological canon of interpretation. This christological canon means: the gospel of free grace and justification through faith alone solely on account of Christ. This is the truly apostolic standard. It cannot be overly stressed that, for Luther, what counted was the material contents of the book and not its formal position within Scripture. Thus, although Luther retained the established canon of the ancient church, he discovered within it a canon by which all its parts could be judged. Luther said:

> All the sacred books agree in this, that all of them preach and inculcate (*treiben*) Christ. And that is the true test by which we judge all books, when we see whether or not they inculcate Christ. For all the Scriptures show us Christ, Romans 3[:21]; and St. Paul will know nothing but Christ, I Corinthians 2 [:2]. Whatever does not teach Christ is not yet apostolic, even though St. Peter or St. Paul does the teaching. Again, whatever preaches Christ would be apostolic, even if Judas, Annas, Pilate, and Herod were doing it.[1]

This "canon within the canon" is not something that Luther brought to the biblical text out of his subjective experience. Rather, it could be found as the clear center of the main books of Scripture itself. In the New Testament the books that most clearly convey Christ are the Gospel of John and the First Letter of John, the epistles of Paul, especially Romans and Galatians, and 1 Peter. The Letter of James is inferior because it preaches law instead of gospel. As for the Revelation of John, Luther stated that he could find no evidence that it was written by the Holy Spirit.

The significant thing is not Luther's critical opinions on various parts of Scripture, but the fact that he applied criticism at all. In the subsequent period of Lutheran orthodoxy, the beginnings of biblical criticism in Luther were virtually aborted. Whereas for Luther the canon was to be found in the Bible, for orthodoxy the canon became equated with the inspired text. Whereas for Luther the material principle of Scripture, namely, justification through faith alone, was primary, for orthodoxy the formal principle of Scripture, namely, that it is verbatim the inspired Word of

God, took precedence. Yet even in the period of orthodoxy some of the dogmaticians continued to make some distinction between the canonical and the deutero-canonical (or apocryphal) books of the New Testatment. Such a distinction had been consistently maintained by all the Reformers with regard to the Old Testament. But now books like 2 Peter, 2 and 3 John, Hebrews, James, Jude, and Revelation were placed in a special class. In general it can be stated that the closer the dogmaticians stood to Luther, the more they preserved the distinction. Thus Martin Chemnitz, representing early Lutheranism, insisted strenuously on the difference between the undoubtedly canonical books and those which had been marked by uncertainty by many in the ancient church as well as by Luther. By the time of David Hollaz, who represents Lutheran orthodoxy in full bloom, the meaning of making any distinction had been lost. This flat, undifferentiated view of the books of the Bible finally triumphed and today survives in Protestant fundamentalism, and there are some Lutherans in this group. The canon which was open and flexible in Luther's thinking became closed and rigid in the circles that inherited the doctrine of Scripture in Protestant orthodoxy.

THE AUTHORITY OF SCRIPTURE

Luther and his fellow Reformers, Zwingli and Calvin, accepted the authority of Scripture. But in this respect they were not manifestly different from their opponents. The theology of the Middle Ages also affirmed the authority of Scripture and its full inspiration. Luther's departure consisted of deriving the authority of Scripture from its gospel content. The gospel is a promise; therefore, for Luther, the Bible is a book of promises that circulated first in the Word of preaching. The living Word of preaching is the basic form of the gospel; the Scriptures are the written form which has become a necessary aid in the ongoing oral proclamation of the church. Luther stated, "However, the need to write books was a serious decline and a lack of the Spirit which necessity forced upon us; it is not the manner of the New Testament."[2]

Luther's decisive break with medieval theology rests on this massive simplification of the manifold character of Scripture: the heart of Scripture is the promise of the gospel that is brought to expression in the Christ event. Its authority is not of a juridical kind; it is not a book of legal doctrines, inerrant reports, or devotional material. The Scriptures convey the life-giving word of salvation in Christ to those who accept it through faith alone. Authority in matters of faith rests on the gospel of Scripture, not on the creeds and councils of the church nor on the hierarchical offices, papacy and episcopacy. The Word of Scripture alone *(sola scriptura)* is to be believed and accepted as finally valid with respect to the concerns of faith and salvation.

Luther's Scripture principle is articulated most clearly in *The Book of Concord* (1580). Although early Lutheranism understood itself as a confessional movement, subscribing to confessions that were authoritative expositions of the truth of Scripture, it never abandoned the principle of the priority of Scripture over confession. Thus the Formula of Concord, Solid Declaration, states: "We pledge ourselves to the prophetic and apostolic writings of the Old and New Testaments as the pure and clear fountain of Israel, which is the only true norm according to which all teachers and teachings are to be judged and evaluated. . . . The Word of God is and should remain the sole rule and norm of all doctrine, and (that) no human being's writings dare be put on a par with it, but (that) everything must be subjected to it."[3]

This same principle was even more clearly elaborated by Zwingli, Calvin, and the confessional documents of the Reformed churches. In none of the Lutheran confessions is there an article explicitly on the authority of Scripture; rather, it is presupposed and applied in implicit terms. However, in the Reformed confessions there are explicit articles on "the Word of God" or "the authority of the Scriptures." Thus, in the *Genevan Confession of Faith* (1536) the very first article deals with Scripture: "We desire to follow Scripture alone as a rule of faith and religion, without mixing it with any other thing which might be devised by the opinion of men, apart from the Word of God." The *Scots Confession* (1560) declares: "As we believe and confess the Scriptures of God sufficient to instruct and make the man of God perfect, so do we affirm and avow the authority of the same to be of God and neither to depend on men or angels. We affirm therefore that such as alleged the Scriptures to have no authority but that which it receives from the Church, to be blasphemous against God and injurious to the true Church." *The Westminster Confession of Faith* (1649) gives a much fuller account of Scripture, stating that the Old Testament in Hebrew and the New Testament in Greek are "immediately inspired by God, and by his singular care and providence kept pure in all ages."

These brief summaries of the early Lutheran and Reformed positions on Scripture indicate two things: (1) that both agree completely on the authority of Scripture, and (2) that the Reformed confessions express a more detailed doctrine of Scripture. In the period of orthodoxy, however, the Lutheran dogmaticians show the same concern as the

Reformed to have a complete doctrine of Scripture. This was due in part to external pressure from the Roman side, which could appeal to a full-fledged doctrine of papal authority, challenging the Protestants to produce one of equal force in the polemical situation. It was also due in part to an interior development in which Luther's stress on the material content of Scripture—justification through faith alone—was given the status of a true doctrinal proposition which, along with others, could be proved from Scripture. In this development the doctrine of the inspiration of Scripture enjoyed a great inflation in the works of the dogmaticians, both Lutheran and Reformed.

In orthodoxy, a shift away from Luther occurs in the account of Scripture's authority. For Luther, as we have seen, the authority of Scripture resides in its gospel content. Scriptures are a means of grace. They are to be judged entirely in terms of Luther's famous formula, *was Christum treibt* ("what conveys Christ"). For the seventeenth-century orthodox dogmaticians, sometimes referred to as scholastics, because they revived the theological methodology of medieval scholasticism, Scriptures are authoritative because of their divine inspiration and inerrancy. Because this doctrine became the official teaching of almost all Lutheran and Reformed churches, and remains valid to this day, except where the historical-critical approach to Scripture has occasioned a new doctrine, it is well to consider some of the essential features of the doctrine of Scripture in Protestant orthodoxy.

The Scriptures are the written deposit of revelation which God communicated to the prophets and apostles by means of the inspiration of the Holy Spirit. God was the real author of Scripture; the human writers were the instruments which God used to produce the Bible. The process of inspiration pertained to both the matter and the form of Scripture. God provided the correct ideas in the minds of the authors, the right words to use, as well as the stimulus on their wills to cause them to write. Hence it follows that, with the Holy Spirit in complete charge of the production of the Scriptures, they are totally free of all errors and imperfections.

The final conclusion to be drawn was that the distinction between the Word of God and the Holy Scriptures, which Luther was able to assert, could be allowed to vanish. The activity of God in the writing of the Bible was so direct that it was likened to dictation. The Holy Spirit dictated in so many words, including punctuation marks, what was to be written down. The prophets, evangelists, and apostles were the inspired secretaries. David Hollaz writes: "All the words, without exception, contained in the Holy Manuscript, were dictated by the Holy Spirit to the pen of the prophets and apostles."[4] The ground of the authority of Scripture was shifted from the gospel revelation to a verbal inspiration. A great fascination arose concerning the miraculous intervention of the Holy Spirit. It was even taught that everything the authors would normally know on their own had to be the subject matter of inspiration, in order to close every possible gap that might arise from human fallibility.

The doctrine of verbal inspiration continued to grow as the controversy with the Roman Catholics continued. All the weapons of Protestantism seemed to hang on this one doctrine—the absolutely inspired text of Scripture, down to the last syllable and punctuation mark. The result was the divinization of the biblical texts, the ascription of attributes which nearly rival the attributes of God himself. The faith and obedience which the New Testament refers to God, his Christ, or his gospel, are now transferred to Scripture as the Word of God. In light of the later criticism that emerges in modern Protestantism, some have bluntly dubbed this as bibliolatry, the failure to distinguish between the worship of God and the devotion to Scripture.

The authority which the Scriptures possess in orthodoxy is of an authoritarian kind, commanding blind faith and obedience. This is so because it is affirmed that they are to be believed not merely because of *what* they say, but purely *because* they say it. The Scriptures are endowed with causative authority so that, in the language of orthodoxy, it is said that the Scriptures create faith and obedience; the Scriptures create assent to the truths to be believed. This type of language indicates that the distinction between the Holy Spirit—who alone, according to classical Christianity, possesses such creative, regenerative, and illuminative power—and the Holy Scriptures has virtually collapsed.

Untiringly the orthodox dogmaticians drew up lists of the attributes of Scripture. They possess infallible truth and the power to interpret themselves correctly; the Hebrew and Greek texts are endowed by the providence of God with incorruptibility; and everything taught in the Bible is perfectly true. The Scriptures, in addition, have the attributes of perfection, perspicuity, and efficacy. The perfection of Scripture means that it is the solid Word of God and instructs us flawlessly in things that pertain to the salvation of humankind. In no way does it have to be supplemented by other sources with regard to the true knowledge of God and his revelation. By the perspicuity of Scripture is meant that it is clear and plain for everyone to understand. No light outside of Scripture needs to be turned on to make its teachings explicit and meaningful. Thus Scripture has the quality of efficacy in itself, that is, "even apart from its use" *(etiam extra usum).*

In the theology of the Reformation we are thus faced with two doctrines of the authority of Scripture. For Luther and Melanchthon and their closest pupils, the authority of Scripture is grounded in the testimony which the law and the gospel imprint in the hearts of believers. The Scripture is to be believed on account of Christ, its essential content. The other doctrine holds that Scripture is trustworthy because of the testimonies that prove its divine origin by means of inspiration. There are traces of this doctrine also in Luther and Melanchthon, which they inherited from a tradition going back to the early church and its Jewish antecedents. Likewise, within the Calvinist Reformed tradition the same two forms of the doctrine of Scripture exist side by side. For Calvin, Scripture's authority is communicated to believers by the internal testimony of the Holy Spirit *(testimonium Spiritus Sancti internum)*; it is an immediate certainty of faith in response to hearing God's Word in Scripture. This is a certainty that only the Spirit can work and cannot be built up inductively by rational proofs. In later Calvinism a biblicism emerges which neglects Calvin's teaching and which petrifies the authority of the Bible in words mechanically dictated by the Holy Spirit.

In both Lutheran and Calvinist orthodoxy, the Scriptures are buttressed with arguments that prove their authority. Testimonies in favor of Scripture and evidences of its divine origin are enumerated, such as the miracles it reports, the antiquity of the writings, the literal fulfillment of the prophecies, the moral superiority of its doctrine in comparison with that of the pagans, the joy of the martyrs, and so on. This doctrine of testimonies for Scripture became the point at which the battle line was drawn between the orthodox defenders of Scripture and the critics of the Enlightenment who sought purely rational proofs for the contents of belief. The reasoning was simple: if the authority of Scripture was to be defended by rational evidences, it could be attacked on the same grounds. And so the Bible became the subject of a long, drawn-out controversy between the supernaturalism of the orthodox party and the naturalism of the biblical critics.

Luther's emphasis on the Bible as the living voice of the gospel enjoyed a revival in Pietism. Pietism may be seen as a counteraction to orthodoxy, insofar as it was less concerned to have a systematic doctrine about Scripture than to read it directly as a means of spiritual experience and growth in Christian living. This brought about an intensification of interest in the study of the Bible. Here we find perhaps the origin of the modern existentialist exegesis of Scripture.

Just as Pietism grew up on the soil of Lutheran orthodoxy, recapturing the existentially personal dimension of Scripture's message (Luther's *pro me*), so also there grew up within Calvinist biblicism a school which read the Bible as a book of history. This is the "federal theology" of John Coccejus (1669), who stressed the history recorded by the Bible as a series of interconnected covenants. This historical conception of the Bible had enormous influence on thinkers like J. G. Herder, J. A. Bengel, J. T. Beck, and J. C. K. von Hofmann, all forerunners of the contemporary history-of-salvation theology *(Heilsgeschichte)*. In this line, the authority of the Bible rests on the meaning of the historical events which the Bible reports. The Bible itself bears witness to this meaning: all the events point to Christ as the midpoint of history. This christocentric view of the Bible again gathers up an emphasis so central in the theology of Luther and Calvin.

The authority of the Bible was the basic presupposition which the Reformation held in common with the Middle Ages as well as with its Roman Catholic contemporaries. But already in the sixteenth century, impulses increased until there was a floodtide of biblical criticism in the Enlightenment that applied the categories of "nature" and "reason" to wash away the foundations of biblical authority. The English deists, the French encyclopedists, and the German thinkers of the Enlightenment released such an avalanche of critical methods and insights that not only was the orthodox theory of verbal inspiration swept away, but the unique status of Scripture in theology and the church was severely threatened. The result is that, in modern theology, the authority of the Bible no longer functions as an unquestioned presupposition as it did in the theology of the Reformers, but is treated precisely as that which has to be established. Biblical authority stands or falls with the approach one takes; it has become a matter of interpretation. In the contemporary idiom, it is a hermeneutical question.

TRADITION AND INTERPRETATION

The churches of the Reformation have always understood themselves as the creation of the ongoing activity of biblical interpretation. In the nature of the case, Luther had to gain leverage from the Bible in his struggle against his opponents who appealed to ecclesiastical tradition and church authority. This single-minded appeal to Scripture set in motion a rich history of discovering new means of grasping the biblical word. Luther's most revolutionary principle of interpretation was the insistence on the literal, historical, and philological exposition of the Scriptures. He thereby rejected the allegorical method of exegesis which had been practiced to excess since Origen. By means of allegorical exegesis, Luther charged, it is possible to prove anything one wishes from Scripture. The effect was to rob Scripture of its own validity and to diminish its power to criticize the evolving traditions of the church. Luther believed that if Scripture was to regain its primacy in the church, the interpretation would have to be bound to the literal sense as that appears in the original Hebrew and Greek texts. So Luther said: "We will not long preserve the gospel without the languages. The languages are the sheath in which this sword of the Spirit is contained (Eph. 6:17)."[5] Against the spiritualists who sought some hidden meanings behind the words of the text, Luther said: "The Holy Spirit is the simplest writer and adviser in heaven and on earth. That is why his words could have no more than the one simplest meaning which we call the written one, or the literal meaning of the tongue."[6]

In addition to his insistence that the biblical expositor must search out the literal sense of Scripture, Luther maintained that every passage has only one authentic meaning. The allegorists had found sometimes as many as four meanings in a verse: the literal, allegorical, moral (tropological), and mystical (anagogical). Luther did away with this complicated apparatus which filled the biblical commentaries of the medieval scholastics with idle and sometimes dangerous speculations. The interpreter must not be the master and judge of Scripture, but only bring to expression Scripture's own witness to itself. It is not the church which authorizes the meaning of Scripture; the Scripture authenticates itself. The church has only to listen and obey. "The gospel is not believed because the church confirms it, but because one recognizes that it is God's word."[7] To those who argued that at least the church determined the canon, Luther retorted that only the Word of God determines what is canonical. Luther stopped at this point. One searches in vain for a further answer to those who counter with the charge that this is circular reasoning, proving one unknown thing by appealing to another unknown thing.

A further step in Luther's hermeneutical position is the principle: "Scripture interprets itself."[8] This means that the standard of interpretation cannot come from outside of Scripture. This principle was applied polemically against both the Roman theologians and the Protestant enthusiasts. The Roman theologians controlled the interpretation of Scripture by the teaching office of the church; the enthusiasts read Scripture in light of their own spiritual experiences. In both cases some standard outside of Scripture was used to determine what was relevant. Either way leads to the erection of some authority alongside of Scripture or above it. Luther's position was that, to be sure, the Spirit of God enables the right interpretation of Scripture. The Spirit, however, does not operate apart from the scriptural word, but is mediated through it. Luther wanted nothing alien to Scripture to be permitted to determine the saving message it communicates.

Such an emphasis on the sovereignty of Scripture did not mean that the tradition of the church was to be rejected. This was not an exclusive biblicism, with no room for the classical creeds, dogmas, and traditions of the church. Martin Chemnitz formulated the classic Lutheran statement on the role and significance of tradition.[9] He observed that there are eight different meanings of tradition and that all of them, except one, are positively affirmed by the Reformation theologians. First, there is the oral tradition of Christ and his apostles written down by the evangelists. Here Scripture and tradition are identical. Second, there is the tradition of handing down the Scriptures from age to age on the part of the church. Third, there are apostolic doctrines referred to by the early fathers which are not written down in Scripture. Fourth, there is the exegetical tradition of expounding the Scriptures. Fifth, there is the tradition of doctrines built up by the church, not taught in Scripture in so many words, but only by implication. Sixth, the term is applied to what is called the tradition of the fathers, the patristic consensus. Seventh, there is the ecclesiastical tradition of rites and customs which are very ancient. They may be observed on account of their antiquity, provided they do not conflict with gospel. Eighth, there are traditions pertaining to faith and morals with no basis in Scripture, but which the Council of Trent commands to be revered with the "same reverence and pious affection" as Scripture itself. In this one last sense, tradition is to be rejected.

The picture that emerges is that the Lutheran Reformation by intent was relatively conservative on tradition, calling for reform only at those points where tradition conflicted with the gospel. The Calvinistic tradition went a step beyond Lutheranism; it was less favorable to the Catholic tradition and earnestly tried to reconstruct the whole church, not only its faith and morals but also its polity and rituals, on the basis of biblical principles. For the Calvinists, Scripture could be treated as a blueprint of the constitution of the church; for the Lutherans, a wide range of freedom was permitted to the developing Catholic tradition so long as the gospel message of Scripture remained clear and central. For this reason the Lutherans did not derive the structure of the church and its form of worship from the New Testament, as the Calvinists tried to do, but were satisfied to retain greater continuity with the established tradition. No wonder that Lutheranism has appeared to other Protestants as a halfway reformation. In the Lutheran self-understanding, however, the Reformation has been from the beginning essentially a matter of the true preaching of the gospel and the right administration of the sacraments; it was not chiefly an institutional and moral reform movement.

The hermeneutics of the orthodox period effected a systematization of the principles of interpretation which Luther applied. The basic premise was the clarity of Scripture; the Bible is not a dark and obscure book that only a few professors can understand. This does not mean that all the passages are clear, only that all that is necessary for Christian faith and life is clearly revealed in Scripture. The rule was followed to clarify the obscure passages in light of the clear and lucid ones. The idea of the clarity of Scripture did not mean that the unregenerate person can grasp the true meaning of Scripture. Without the aid of the Holy Spirit, we can understand the words and syntax, but the real saving content of Scripture will elude us until our hearts are tuned in to the Spirit. The true interpretation of Scripture is a gift of faith worked by the Holy Spirit. This was finally taken to mean the ability to hold fast to what Scripture says even if it means a break with reason and runs contrary to the evidence of the senses. It may, indeed, require a *sacrificium intellectus.*

With the full emergence of biblical criticism in the age of the Enlightenment, the pillars of orthodox hermeneutics were attacked and shattered. Yet the biblical critics, who applied the new methods of literacy and historical analysis, conceived of their work as faithful to Luther's own pioneering critical insights. They could appeal to Luther's critical statements about certain books of the Bible. However, unlike Luther, they did not apply a canon of criticism from within Scripture itself, namely, the free gift of justifying grace on account of Christ, but developed an autonomous scientific criticism of the biblical documents. The methods of historical-critical investigation which were applied to all ancient writings are now applied without hesitation to the biblical writings. The history of the development and refinement of the historical-critical method covers the last two centuries and is very complex, so that we can only highlight several of its main features.[10]

The basic premise of the new criticism was that the orthodox doctrine of inspiration has no heuristic validity at all in the scholarly study of the Bible. The investigation must proceed without prejudice concerning the special authority of this book. The biblical writings are products of two thousand years of history and must be examined as are all other literary remains from antiquity. The startling discovery was that the ecclesiastical dogmas were not to be found in the Bible but were products of a later time. In the age of Christendom the dogmas of the Trinity and Christ, as formulated in the Nicene and Athanasian Creeds, were necessary to believe for salvation. Now the biblical critics could apply the Scripture principle of Protestantism to show that these dogmas are not required for faith since they lack solid biblical support. One of the main incentives in the history of criticism was in fact to achieve freedom for scholarly research from the oppressive authority of the church and its dogmatic controls. If the dogmas could be undermined, no field of research could be declared off-limits.

Three areas of research involving the interpretation of Scripture brought the new criticism into virulent conflict with traditional modes of understanding. First of all, there was the criticism of the Gospels, which are the main source documents of the birth, ministry, and death of Jesus of Nazareth. The overall result of Gospel criticism was shocking to those whose faith was dependent on the utter reliability of every word of Scripture. For the words and deeds of Jesus which the Gospels report were at least intermingled with and modified by the beliefs of the early church. The question of who Jesus of Nazareth really was and what he accomplished became a matter of research and, therefore, always in principle an open question subject to continuing investigation. This research affected the christological dogma because it placed in question the traditional assertion of the divinity of Christ and the notion that a person's relation to God was determined by what he or she believed about Jesus of Nazareth.

Second, the unity of the New Testament was challenged on the grounds that there were different and rival theologies circulating in primitive Christianity. The theology of John is different from the theology of Luke, and Paul's theology is very different again. The upshot of this finding was to challenge the idea that the unity of the church could be founded on the unity of doctrine since in the New Testament itself there is a plurality of theologies. This led to the relativizing of church dogma and the traditional demand for a *consensus doctrinae.*

Third, critics were eager to show that the biblical documents are not unique, but reflect the religious ideas of their environment. The teachings of Jesus were traced back into various strands of Judaism, and the Christianity of the Pauline and Johannine congregations was regarded as an expression of the religious syncretism of late antiquity.

In view of these critical results, the question was bound to arise: What then is the ground and content of Christian faith? What is the essential core of the New Testament that defines the essence of Christianity for each succeeding generation? Is an absolutely objective answer to this question possible? A critical investigation of the history of biblical criticism indicates, as Albert Schweitzer documented so clearly in *The Quest of the Historical Jesus*, that each epoch reads and interprets the Bible through the spectacles of its own milieu and world view. Eighteenth-century rationalism was able to portray Jesus as a teacher of moral enlightenment, espousing the eternal truths of rational religion. In the nineteenth century the Tübingen School of F. C. Baur interpreted the New Testament under the spell of Hegel's dialectical philosophy of history. Thus, history is the dialectical unfolding of a religious idea; in the New Testament this idea clothed itself in the christological symbols of that day. In due time it is possible to dispense with the outer symbolic language in favor of the pure concept stated philosophically. David F. Strauss shocked the Christian world with his *Life of Jesus*, in which he broke through the supernaturalism on the right and the rationalistic naturalism on the left, and projected the mythological hypothesis. The New Testament should be interpreted in terms of its mythical character. The point is not to argue whether the miracles happened or how they could be explained in natural terms, but to see that myth was the language of religion of that time. It is the nature of myth to speak of the otherworldly in terms of this world; therefore, it is pointless to ask whether the myths convey historical facts.

Protestant liberalism in the nineteenth century provides numerous examples of a strange admixture of two tendencies. On the one hand, the biblical critics were zealous in their commitment to scientific historical scholarship; on the other hand, their religious commitments and philosophical presuppositions shone through all their critical scholarship. In spite of trying to be utterly historical, they found themselves reading the ideas of their own time into the biblical documents. The school of Albrecht Ritschl is a case in point. The Ritschlians were deeply influenced by the Kantian moral philosophy of religion. They looked for the ethical superiority of Christianity; they tended to interpret Jesus as a religious personality who had the power to enkindle a like religiosity in others. Harnack called theology away from the religion about Jesus, as we find in Paul, to the simple religion of Jesus, as he himself believed and taught it. Thus his famous assertion: "The Gospel, as Jesus proclaimed it, has to do with the Father only and not with the Son."[11] By the end of the nineteenth century the critical movement in theology had stimulated a crisis over the Scripture principle in the very church that boasted of being the church of the Word of God.

THE USES OF SCRIPTURE

It is a well-established fact of church history that the practice of the church is often better than its theology. Orthopraxy does not always derive strictly from orthodoxy. So has it been with respect to the use of the Scriptures in the Reformation churches. The Reformation gave to Scripture its prominent place not only as the unique source of theology, but also as the chief resource of preaching and worship. The practical use of the Bible in personal devotion and in liturgical worship has been the main impetus to update the translation of the Bible in every age. To be sure, there has always been a resistance to the attempt to render the biblical texts in modern speech. The defense of the King James Version in the Anglo-Saxon world and of Luther's Bible in Germany has been strong precisely because their renderings have been so firmly fixed in the pious consciousness of the masses. The churches of the Reformation have read portions of the Holy Bible in every worship service for the last 450 years.

Particularly in the Lutheran churches, the historic system of reading appointed lessons for the day, called pericopes, has been accepted from the beginning. This is a system that dates back before Charlemagne's time, A.D. 800. It follows the basic structure of the church year, broken into segments by the observance of the great festivals. Generally one lesson was read from the Old Testament, one from the epistles, and one from the Gospels. Together they were recognized as determining the theme of the day, suggesting the subject of the sermon, and providing stimulation for the writing of new hymns and melodies to carry the biblical message. The Zwinglian and the Calvinist churches abandoned the pericope system altogether, leaving it up to each congregation and each preacher to work out their own way through the year. In more recent times there has been a trend on the part of these Protestant churches to reconstruct the church year in some fashion that approaches the traditional structure. In this way the church universal is united in worship in each of its congregational embodiments rather than being atomized by the religious predilections of its preachers. The system, when used diligently, makes it less likely that preachers will ride their hobbyhorses every Sunday and punish the faithful with their own religious ideas.

In addition to liturgical use, Protestant Christians have encouraged the devotional reading of the Bible. This personalist approach to the Bible has been practiced especially in the evangelical revivalist wings of Protestant Christianity. The individual reads each day a portion of Scripture which is not necessarily related to any particular problem or topic of research, but is selected pretty much at random. The words of the Bible are studied not with the intention of mining their original meaning, but with an interest in the impressions they make on the soul of the reader. The attitude is not critically objective, but receptively subjective. The controlling medium of reflection is not historical but psychological. Another technique has been to memorize Bible verses, filing them away in the back of the mind so that they are ready for instant recall to meet the needs of the hour.

The Bible has also functioned in the Reformation churches as a book of instruction, especially in the training of the clergy. The method of study is usually a combination of historical principles, theological implications, and practical applications. The Bible is the book of the church, and is not just for the use of the individual Christian. The Reformation churches have on the whole maintained a positive churchly approach to the Scriptures, succumbing neither to the atomism of scientific historical-criticism nor to the arbitrariness of the individualistic psychological method. The Scriptures have been expounded as a canon that guides, supports, and determines the proclamation and doctrine of the church. In turn, the historical confession of the church guides the individual interpreters of the Bible. Thus the church's confession of faith is an element of the context that biblical exegetes bring to their study of Scripture.

The controlling interest of the theologian is not primarily historical, nor is it psychological; rather, it relates to the life of the church, its ministry of proclamation, and its mission in the world. The Bible has been used, therefore, as the basic text of both the teaching office and the preaching office of the church. In this churchly approach, the theologian does not ask, "What does the Bible have to say *to me*?", but "What does the Bible say to the churches also in our time?" In this way the authority of the Bible is not so much an attribute of the book in itself but a dynamic quality that is demonstrated in the process of the church's use of it. The test of the church's attitude toward the Bible has not actually been the "high" doctrine of Scripture it has been able to construct, but the extent to which the Bible is used in the building up of the church, in preaching, instruction, and mission. Every new reformation in the churches of the Reformation has been invariably triggered by a revival of biblical study. The ongoing reformation of the church is linked to the use of the Bible as the medium of divine revelation.

THE BIBLE IN CONTEMPORARY THEOLOGY

In contemporary Protestantism the burning issue continues to be how to unify the historical and hermeneutical approaches to the Bible. The purely historical interest can stifle the concern for the relevance of the biblical message today; the purely hermeneutical concern can force the Scripture into the mold of modern questions, so that the historical horizon of its own message tends to be neglected. The attempt to take the message of the Bible on its own terms and make it speak prophetically to the current situation received a special impetus in the neo-Reformation theology of Karl Barth and Emil Brunner just after World War I. The appropriate name for this movement is the "theology of the Word of God." These theologians took the Bible with a renewed seriousness, thinking of themselves as disciples of Luther and Calvin. Almost all of the more recent currents in Protestant theology owe the vital role of biblical studies in dogmatic and systematic theology to Karl Barth.

In Barth's theology, the Word of God is the central concept. The Word of God comes to us in a threefold form: the preached Word, the written Word, and the revealed Word. The Word is by nature correspondingly speech, deed, and mystery—a threefoldness which is present in each of the forms of the Word of God. All three forms and aspects are the one Word of God. This threeness-in-oneness and this oneness-in-threeness provide the only analogy to the doctrine of the Holy Trinity.

The Word of God is not a remote word of antiquity; it is the Word heard in the proclamation of the church today. This motif is a recurrence of Luther's stress on preaching from the Bible. The church preaches the Word which is a witness to Christ, the revealed Word. This revealed Word proclaimed in the living language of the church is attested to by the Word of Scripture. Thus the three forms—preaching, revelation, and Scripture—converge on the one name of Jesus Christ, in whom God reveals himself as the Lord of the world. These themes of the Word of God are developed and repeated in the many volumes of Barth's *Church Dogmatics* and from there have found their way into many branches of the modern church, including Eastern Orthodoxy and Roman Catholicism.

The controversy over the Bible was not settled in the eighteenth and nineteenth centuries. An enormous gap has opened up within the Christian denominations regarding the interpretation of Scripture. In most denominations there is an attempt to recover the authority of the Bible in precisely the terms it enjoyed in seventeenth-century orthodoxy, that is, before the rise of biblical criticism. Fundamentalist biblicism has not receded in vigor even though it does not enjoy much prestige in the great theological schools of this epoch. Masses of the laity as well as the clergy wish to possess an uncomplicated answer to the question of authority. Biblicism holds to an infallible Bible that can be the absolute authority in matters of belief and morals. The ancient doctrine of verbal inspiration survives. In some Christian groups the theory of inspiration is used to vouch for the absolute reliability of the Bible on all matters which relate to cosmology, biology, geography, chronology, and history. The Bible is used as a bulwark against the evolutionary hypothesis of modern natural science. The authority of Scripture, for Luther and his followers, was affirmed with respect to its chief purpose of declaring the gospel of Christ for faith and salvation; in modern Protestant fundamentalism, which ironically claims to bear the legacy of the Reformation, the authority of Scripture is extended to include infallible information on all kinds of subjects.

Fundamentalist biblicism is rejected by most theologians, and is out of favor in most of the seminaries that train clergy for the parish ministry. They reject biblicism not merely because historical science has disclosed errors and contradictions in the biblical writings but because biblicism elevates the authority of the Bible to the point that the authority of Christ and his gospel is eclipsed. The non-fundamentalist Protestants also accept the Bible as the Word of God in some sense, but they point out that the concept of the Word of God, as Barth made clear, cannot be confined to the Bible. They cannot say that the Bible is the Word of God in a simplistic way, for the concept of the Word of God bears many diverse meanings in the classical Christian tradition.

Paul Tillich has observed that the Word of God has six meanings.[12] First of all, the Word of God refers classically to the second person of the Trinity, who was coeternal with the Father. Second, the Word of God was the active agent and medium of the creation of the world. Third, the Word of God was preached by the prophets in the Old Testament. Fourth, the Word of God became flesh in the person of Jesus of Nazareth. Fifth, the Word of God was proclaimed by the apostles of Jesus Christ in creating the church. Later it was written down by the apostles and their disciples. The Bible is the written Word of God in a derived way; it is the deposit of the preaching of the early church. Sixth, the Word of God is the living voice of the gospel in every generation of Christians to follow. In light of these perspectives it appears that the Protestant fundamentalist doctrine of Scripture represents a reduction of the Word of God to its written form.

A corollary of the revival of the Reformation theology of the Word of God has been the christological interpretation of Scripture. The christocentricity of Barth's theology has made an enormous impact on modern biblical theology. All of the meanings of the Word of God have one center and norm: the appearance of Jesus Christ in history. For neo-orthodox Christians following this line the ultimate authority in matters of faith and life must be the Word of God who was made flesh, who died and rose again for the salvation of humanity. The honor of his name is mediated through Scripture and now lives through his Spirit in the Christian community today. The humanity of God in Christ is emphasized as well as the historicity of all the means of his self-communication. The Word of God is not apart from humanity; rather, God uses human words and concepts, human hands and lips, human history in its glory and tragedy. The medium of his revelation is completely incarnational.

Modern Protestant theology continues to show a marked preference for stressing the humanity of God in Christ in the spirit of Luther, who insisted that one can never draw God's Son too deeply into human flesh. The Scriptures, both Old and New Testaments, are Christ-centered; they point to the revelation of God in Jesus Christ. The theme of the Bible is: He must increase! This means that the Scriptures cannot be exalted above Christ. The creeds and confessions of the church cannot supplement the final self-revelation of God in Jesus of Nazareth. Personal religious experience cannot add any stature to the magnitude of the Christ event.

The uniqueness, the authority, and the value of the Bible therefore continue to be central in modern Protestant Christianity. By means of Scripture, Christ is pictured and proclaimed as God's message and answer to the human predicament. Subsidiary to this central idea, the Bible is treated as a collection of ancient documents which give us information about the history of Israel and the beginnings of Christianity. The Bible is appreciated as a library of great literature, ranking with the greatest literature of the ancient world from a humanist, literary-critical viewpoint. The Bible is a source document for the imaginative construction of church doctrines; it provides fresh stimulus in every age to create new history in the realm of doctrine. The Bible is a devotional book full of inspiring passages to cultivate the religious life. But, beyond all these viewpoints, the Bible is the unique book of the church because of its original and intrinsic connection with the history of the promises of God and its astonishing denouement in the career of Jesus the Christ.

It is finally for the sake of Christ alone that the church continues to regard the Bible as a book without equal in the history of human literature. For this reason the churches that claim the heritage of Luther and the Reformation still affirm the Bible as the Word of God. This is not meant in the fundamentalistic sense that everything in the Bible stands directly as the Word of God; nor is it meant in the sense that only some things in the Bible are the Word of God, such as the red-lettered passages in some New Testaments or the most inspiring verses of anyone's choosing. The Bible is the Word of God as a whole, in its total import and impact, because it conveys the message of eschatological salvation.

This valuation of the Bible as the Word of God is asserted today with greater difficulty than in Luther's time and with greater awareness of the historical problems involved in biblical interpretation. First of all, the theological task is not so easily limited to the interpretation of the Bible, as it was for Luther. The God to whom Scriptures attest as Creator and Lord of all is active in all spheres of life and human experience. Therefore, whatever theology asserts about God on the basis of Scripture has in some way to be correlated with what can be learned about God's world in nature and history from other disciplines. Theology that attempts to be true to Scripture tries to relate all things to the God of the Bible, to the God of history and of all people and of the entire world from the beginning to its future fulfillment. Modern Protestant theology is currently rediscovering and applying the universal perspective of the Bible, reasserting the implications of the monotheistic idea of God. It faces the challenge of overcoming the dichotomy between theology and the secular sciences, as the world of nature and history that the Bible talks about could hardly be separate from the world that science explores with its different methods.

The role of the Bible in constructive theology is radically qualified today by historical consciousness. Luther held to the univocal sense of Scripture; basically he believed that its literal meaning is identical with its historical content. In other words, things happened exactly as they were written. Today it is impossible to assume the literal historicity of all things recorded. What the biblical authors report is not accepted as a literal transcript of the actual course of events. Therefore, all critical scholars inquire behind the text and attempt to reconstruct the actual history that took place. In Christology this has led to the endless debates on the relation between the historical Jesus and the Christ of apostolic faith and preaching. This debate continues, and there seems to be no way to proceed except to make all Christology an interpretation of the historical Jesus. Otherwise history and interpretation fall asunder, and theology ignores the wisdom of Kant's dictum that all concepts without percepts are empty and all percepts without concepts are blind.

Modern hermeneutics has expanded in scope and significance in order to come to grips with the historical problem of the distance between the historical events and the written testimonies to those events. The Reformation principle that Scripture alone must interpret Scripture—*Scriptura est suipsius interpres*—is broadened to mean that the biblical texts can only be interpreted out of their historical contexts. Critical attention to the historical situation has magnified the sense of the distance between biblical and modern times. The Bible's thought world and its symbols and myths are felt to be utterly different from the modern ways of thinking. Therefore, Bultmann's call to demythologize the biblical concepts is an attempt to interpret the biblical message in terms that people today can understand without taking offense at the alien modes of thought one encounters in the Bible.

Luther's principle of sticking to the single grammatical, historical sense of each portion of Scripture is also applied in modern hermeneutics, but with a different result. Critical attention to what the texts actually say has exploded the notion that a system of orthodox dogmatics can be mined out of Scripture. There are different theological tendencies and teachings in the various texts. Ecumenically this has led to the practical conclusion that the traditional demand for a complete consensus of doctrine may be wrongheaded, if even the Scriptures fail to contain such a consensus. Perhaps the unity of the church can be realized without the kind of doctrinal uniformity demanded by the sixteenth-century theologians on both the Protestant and Catholic sides. In any case, the interpretation of the texts of Scripture can no longer be dominated by the history of dogma so that the exegetes are compelled to produce the proofs the dogmaticians require. Biblical theology and dogmatic theology are not reducible to each other. This awareness is a result of taking the historical development seriously. A deep gulf exists between the biblical world of thought and that of, say, Alexandria in the third century, Rome in the thirteenth, Wittenberg in the sixteenth, or Chicago in the twentieth century. It is the task of hermeneutics to make an intelligible transmission of meaning from the biblical text to the completely new situation here and now. This is a shared task. Theology plays a part, but so also do preaching and worship as well as the faith and the witness of every lay person. For Christianity is not merely the ideas handed down from Scripture, but the life and action of Christ's people in the world. The interpretation of Scripture is not successfully confined to the academic situation; the really creative insights come out of the crucible of missionary experience as the witnesses of Christ take upon themselves the burdens of people today and the pain of the world.

SOLA SCRIPTURA

Contemporary theology gives alternative accounts of biblical authority.[13] But this is not merely something to be deplored. We are actually richer for all the pluralism in theology. For Barth the Bible is authoritative because it is the Word of God's self-revelation. For Cullmann and the whole school of biblical theology, the Bible is authoritative because it is the record of God's history of salvation. For Bultmann the Bible is authoritative because its kerygma announces the Christ event and generates the new self-understanding of faith. For Tillich the Bible is authoritative because its leading symbols participate in the original revelation on which Christianity stands and still answer the questions implied in existence, life, and history today. For Pannenberg the Bible's authority is based on the facts and interpretations of history which its traditions transmit, proleptically grasping the final meaning of universal history. For liberation theology the Bible is authoritative because its paradigm events, from exodus to resurrection, inaugurate the process of liberation which is still going on in the world in the struggles of poor and oppressed peoples. The problem of biblical authority is not that we are confronted by these richly diverse perspectives on the meaning of the Bible for today. We can learn something from a plurality of different ways of reading the Bible, none of them reducible to the other.

The problem of the Bible's authority does not lie in the fact that it can be laid open to all kinds of scientific and scholarly inspection.[14] Nor does it lie in the multiplicity of its contents—chronicles, commandments, laws, stories, myths, poetry, songs, legends, sermons, proverbs, prophecies, aphorisms, letters, prayers, visions, and what not. Nor is it because of historical relativism and the predicament of perspectivism, the fact that each of us sees things out there, as it were, from a moving train.

There are two dialectically related truths which define the necessary conditions for making sense of holding to biblical authority. The acknowledgment of these two conditions will not remove the problem of the Bible. The Bible will always be a problem to the church and theology by virtue of its dangerous message. But once we see the underlying conditions of biblical authority, then we already have in principle the answer to whether Scripture can and must still serve as authority for theology.

The first condition of biblical authority, to start with the subjective pole, is that the Bible be used by the church to define its identity and mission in the world, its being and doing as the community which calls itself Christian. Where there is no church, there is no Bible and no need for it. This is why the Bible can only be studied as Holy Scripture within the context of the church. Minus the fact of the church, the Bible is only an arbitrary collection of documents coming out of the past, essentially on a par with other collections. The Bible is what it is acknowledged to be as such only where the Word is preached and the sacraments are administered. For the church or any part of its theology not to acknowledge the authority of the Bible is plainly self-contradictory and suicidal. For without the Bible there is no other foundational point of reference by which the church can find a word basic to its identity and mission. It is this ecclesial character of the Bible which must be acknowledged; otherwise it makes no sense to speak of biblical authority. The Bible forms the church, and the church has the Bible. The church is in the Bible and the Bible is in the church. The church produced the Bible and the Bible produces the church. Scriptures witness to the church, and the church witnesses to the Scriptures. In this dialectical relationship, the church makes room for the Bible as a norm for its ongoing life. The church very early in its history accepted the Bible as the *norma non normata* for its entire future life and mission. This was the church's way of binding itself to a given revelation, not open to any new revelation above and beyond what the Scripture mediates.

The second condition of biblical authority has to do with the objective pole of Scripture's unifying material content. The authority of the Bible as the church's book is centered in the authority of the church's Lord. All of the various contemporary perspectives on biblical authority can be drawn together as witness to the reality and presence of the Lord Jesus Christ. What does the church know about God's self-revelation (Barth) apart from Christ? Or what is the meaning of salvation history (Cullmann) without Christ as its midpoint? Or what is the content of the apostolic kerygma (Bultmann) apart from the Christ event? Or what is the meaning of all the biblical symbols (Tillich) apart from their connection to their normative center in the new being in Jesus as the Christ? Or how is the unifying end of universal history (Pannenberg) revealed apart from the proleptic event of Jesus' resurrection from the dead? For the Christian church and all individual believers the ultimate authority of the Bible depends on its witness to Jesus Christ, who lived, died, and rose again for the world's salvation, and who lives through Word and Spirit in the world today.

It is on account of Christ that the church confesses the authority of the Bible. The Scriptures are Christ-centered. Luther's old dictum, *was Christum treibt*, is still the best way to speak most clearly of the Bible's authority. Other contemporary ways to account for biblical authority do not deny this, but at best enhance the deeper dimensions of the original and intrinsic connection of the biblical witness to the history of the promises of God and their focal point in the person of Jesus the Christ. According to this witness, true authority and true freedom coincide in Jesus Christ. The truly free person is a slave to Jesus Christ; and to be free is to confess that Jesus is the Messiah of Israel, the Lord of the church, and the Savior of the world.

By stressing these two conditions, the ecclesial context and the christological content, we have unified what came apart in the conflict between Reformation and Roman Catholic Christianity. Roman Catholic doctrine has emphasized that Scripture is a product of the church in a fundamental way. Today every Protestant theologian will grant that the New Testament, for example, is a document that records the faith of primitive Christianity. Taking up the Catholic claim, we can acknowledge that Scripture is already the result of the earliest traditions of the church, generated by its life of preaching and worship. Protestants have had to learn the hard lesson of not setting Scripture against tradition, because Scripture overlaps tradition in the early church. Without this common ground the church would never have been able to determine the cutoff point where tradition congeals into the canon of Scripture, so that the church can declare its whole future as bound to Scripture as to no other segment of its tradition.

Evangelical Reformation doctrine has emphasized that the living witness of the church and its faith is never finally to its own tradition as such, but ultimately to that eschatological revelation of God in Jesus Christ which has been handed down by a succession of apostolic witnesses. That living tradition of apostolic Christianity became authoritative Scripture, *norma non normata*, for the future church and its future understanding of the faith. There is no later teaching office in the church that can credibly place itself above or on a par with Scripture as the norm of norms. But Scripture is not a norm outside of the church; it functions as the norm—conveying the Word, communicating the Spirit, awakening faith—only within the context of the preaching and worship of the concrete church.

We have proposed an evangelical catholic doctrine of biblical authority that is self-consciously continuous with Luther's gospel-centered thrust. It is a position that can still claim *sola scriptura* but not as a battle cry *against* the church and its tradition. Rather, *sola scriptura* means that everything essential in the original apostolic preaching which founded the church is written down in Scripture, and that no later tradition can negate or supersede it. But this apostolic faith and preaching continue to make new history, creating new traditions, just as this has been going on for two thousand years. Some of these traditions are still alive, others are dead; some are powerful, others faintly remembered; some are gospel-bearing, others gospel-alienating, and so on. When the question arises as to which is which—which of the traditions of Christianity really belong to the gospel and which may as well be forgotten—then we (both evangelicals and catholics) have no other recourse than to measure things by the norm in Scripture. There is no teaching office in the church that can give a decisive answer to any question of faith and morals which does not ground its teaching in the common norm of all Christianity, and that is conveyed by Scripture alone. In this sense we can and must still maintain the principle of *sola scriptura*.

NOTES

1. "Preface to the Epistles of St. James and St. Jude 1546 (1522)." *Luther's Works*, American Edition, Philadelphia and St. Louis (hereafter referred to as *LW*), 35:396.

2. "The Gospel for the Festival of the Epiphany," *LW* 52:206.

3. Formula of Concord, Solid Declaration, Summary Formulation 3 and 19, *The Book of Concord*, trans. and ed. Theodore G. Tappert (Philadelphia: Fortress Press, 1959), pp. 503-5.

4. Quoted in a reprint of Heinrich Schmid, *The Doctrinal Theology of the Evangelical Lutheran Church* (Minneapolis: Augsburg Publishing House, 1961), p. 45.

5. "To the Councilmen of All Cities in Germany that They Establish and Maintain Christian Schools," *LW* 45:360.

6. "Answer to the Hyperchristian, Hyperspiritual, and Hyperlearned Book by Goat Emser," *LW* 39:178.

7. Quoted by Paul Althaus, *The Theology of Martin Luther*, trans. Robert C. Schultz (Philadelphia: Fortress Press, 1966), p. 75.

8. Ibid., p. 76.

9. Martin Chemnitz, *Examination of the Council of Trent*, Part I, trans. Fred Kramer (St. Louis: Concordia Publishing House, 1971), pp. 223-307.

10. Cf. Edgar Krentz, *The Historical-Critical Method* (Philadelphia: Fortress Press, 1975).

11. Adolf von Harnack, *What is Christianity?* (New York: Harper & Brothers, 1957), p. 144.

12. Paul Tillich, *Systematic Theology*, (Chicago: University of Chicago Press, 1951), 1:157-59.

13. David Kelsey has demonstrated this fact in *The Uses of Scripture in Recent Theology* (Philadelphia: Fortress Press, 1975).

14. Cf. the current reexamination of the role of the historical-critical method in theology and church set in motion by Brevard S. Childs' *Introduction to the Old Testament as Scripture* (Philadelphia: Fortress Press, 1979). In German, Peter Stuhlmacher has formulated a trenchant critique of the historical-critical method, its results and presuppositions. Cf. Peter Stuhlmacher, *Historical Criticism and Theological Interpretation: Toward a Hermeneutics of Content*, trans. Roy A. Harrisville (Philadelphia: Fortress Press, 1977).

2 The Confessional Principle

THE CONFESSIONAL FACTOR IN CHRISTIAN FAITH

Lutheranism has been from the beginning a confessional movement, and present trends indicate that all Lutheran communities around the world intend to continue their life and mission on a confessional basis. The movement toward unity in American Lutheranism continues to stimulate interest in the Lutheran confessional heritage. Lutherans have traditionally insisted on doctrinal consensus as a condition of church unity. Before Lutherans unite even among themselves, it is common practice to ground that unity on a common affirmation of faith elaborated in clear doctrinal statements. A non-confessional Christianity is a contradiction in terms and cannot exist for long. It becomes a cut-flower Christianity, bound to wither and die under the heat of competing religious and ideological movements. As long as there has been a Christian church, it has bound itself to some basic confessions, such as: Jesus is the Christ, Jesus is Lord, Jesus is God and Savior. There has never been a pure kerygma void of doctrinal substance. Thus, when Lutherans focus on their confessional writings, gathered together in an ecumenically intimidating volume, *The Book of Concord*, they are drawing out the implications of the confessional factor given in the basic fact of faith itself. Other Christian groups may at times feel that Lutherans overwork their confessional principle, but actually every body of Christians "believes, teaches, and confesses" some definite things in response to the way the Word of God has addressed them. Moreover, every group uses some instrument to draw the limits of fellowship somewhere. Consider, for example, the nonconfessional evangelicals in America; they refuse to join the World Council of Churches and exclude themselves from the mainline ecumenical movement for their own doctrinal reasons. Without clarifying their claims in clear confessional statements, these so-called evangelicals often fall prey to prejudice and slander their fellow Christians.

The confessional datum of faith is most clearly seen in the baptismal formulae and eucharistic hymns that make up the most primitive creeds of Christianity. And what the church confessed before *God in worship* soon became the substance of what it declared to the *world in witness*. That world may be secular or religious, and the form of that witness may be kerygmatic, didactic, apologetic, and even polemic. The classical trinitarian and christological definitions of the ecumenical creeds interweave many of these elements. Our particular Lutheran confessional writings affirm the classical creeds and in fact presuppose their contents. It is not surprising that the Lutheran tradition, committed to the ecumenical creeds and its own confessional documents, would be second to none in the art of interpreting the Christian faith in voluminous systems of dogmatics.

In the nineteenth century it became common to say, especially in the Marburg School, whose leaders were the great theologians in the Kant-Ritschl line—Wilhelm Herrmann and Adolf von Harnack—that dogma is a specifically Catholic notion which entered Christianity by way of the intellectualizing process of Hellenization, and that this notion of a dogmatic Christianity was one the Protestant Reformation regrettably did not succeed in overcoming. In the twentieth century, Lutheran theologians have reversed this verdict and recognize that there is something both right and wrong in such an assessment. It is true that there is a specifically Roman Catholic concept of dogma as revealed truths (*dogmata revelata*) which are infallibly guaranteed by the magisterium. This is a heteronomous concept of dogma which contradicts the sense of the gospel. But it is equally true that dogma may serve as a watchful witness to the gospel, protecting it from every alienating synthesis.

It is important for Lutheran self-understanding to acknowledge that its confessional principle functions within the framework of the Catholic tradition, affirming a strong sense of dogma, and is not the starting point of a new Christianity. Our Lutheran confessions presuppose the ecumenical dogmas. If Lutheran confessionalism were to establish itself independently of a Catholic consensus, we would have nothing but the making of a new sect. We do not deny, of course, that empirically speaking it has often worked the other way: the more confessional, the more sectarian. But that is an aberration that falls to our generation to correct. The true intent of the Lutheran confessional heritage is to settle for nothing less than a theonomous vision of a church with an evangelical heart beating in a Catholic body. By origin and present self-understanding, Lutherans combine the evangelical confessional principle with the tradition of Catholic dogma. This is what Paul Tillich meant by distinguishing but not separating "Protestant principle" and "Catholic substance."

THE PROBLEM OF CONFESSIONAL IDENTITY

In spite of their confessional heritage, Lutherans have struggled like other Christian groups with the problem of their own identity. What is Lutheranism? What is *authentic* Lutheranism? Some must be committing forgery, writing bad checks on the Lutheran account. As Lutherans we have no magisterium that can impose an answer from above. Lutherans have frequently reacted to this dilemma of self-definition by claiming to take the confessions more seriously than all the others, thus becoming the "scribes and Pharisees" of a Lutheran sect. Peter Brunner put his finger on this wound in world Lutheranism when he wrote about the ecclesiological problem of the Lutheran World Federation. "It can be stated in this way," he said. "Despite the express affirmation of the doctrinal basis, it is doubted that a *consensus* with respect to the doctrine of the gospel actually exists among the churches joined together in the World Federation."[1] Lutherans now separated do not trust the sincerity of each other's confessional subscription. For some people mere confessional subscription is not enough; it must be done "seriously." Some require as a condition of "altar and pulpit fellowship" a certain amount of confessional good works. It is ironic that a church can become absolutely legalistic about a set of documents that condemns all legalism and not see the point.

The fact is that Lutherans today do not know how to offer a clear answer to the question, What is Lutheranism? They seem confused about whether they are looking for a descriptive or a normative answer. Many Lutherans have experienced, furthermore, that they stand closer to certain Protestant denominations and Roman Catholic communities than they do to others who bear the same label. At many points the older confessional issues have been transcended by the twentieth-century clash between fundamentalism and modernism. Some Lutherans, claiming to be confessional, are actually indistinguishable from fundamentalists.

We can discern various attitudes among Lutherans to our confessional heritage. There are at least five types:

1. The first is the attitude of repristination. The basic aim of this type of Lutheran confessionalism is to repristinate the theology of orthodox Lutheranism. The assumption is that the doctrinal development from Luther through the sixteenth-century confessions and seventeenth-

century orthodoxy is homogeneous. It is supposedly the task of present-day Lutheranism to model its thinking after the pristine form of original Lutheranism and repeat it for our generation. This conservative, repristinatory approach has reacted to the cooling off of confessional ardor in more liberal segments of Lutheranism by demanding a legalistic pledge of subscription to the book of confessions. The confessional statements are then applied as rules and laws to govern what ministers and officers of the church say publicly.

2. A second type of attitude is that of liberal nonconfessional Lutheranism, typical of some leading Lutheran scholars of the nineteenth century. This position leaps backward over the period of seventeenth-century orthodoxy and *The Book of Concord* to the creative years of the young reformer, Martin Luther. Luther becomes a hero of the cult of Protestantism. Much of the best Luther research has undoubtedly been inspired by the desire to undercut the normative role of seventeenth-century categories and to gain the leverage of Luther for modern interests. It is much easier to modernize Luther than to try to prove the relevance of "The Formula of Concord" or Lutheran scholasticism. Wilhelm Herrmann, for example, in his great work, *The Communion of the Christian with God,* set forth his theology of moral experience as a reflection on Luther's experience of faith.

3. A third approach may be called hypothetical confessional Lutheranism. The basic motive of this position is to take history seriously and to accept the implications of historical relativism. According to this view, our modern situation has been so drastically modified by the revolutions in the natural and historical sciences that any confessional statements conceived in a prescientific age can no longer be ours in a direct way. Nevertheless, it is claimed, we may still accept these confessions as part of our heritage, as symbols of our origins. Moreover, these confessions are still ours in a hypothetical sense. Were we to confront the same issues as our Lutheran forefathers, we would adopt their identical positions. Lutherans today would still fight Roman sacerdotalism and Zwinglian sacramentarians in the way the sixteenth-century confessors did. We could have been among the subscribers "without reservation." But, of course, times have changed; and so there are certain strings attached to our confessional loyalty. This is a new version of the old *quatenus* formula. *Quatenus* means "insofar as." People espousing the *quatenus* formula could accept the confessions only "insofar as" they conform to Scripture. This is a deficient form of subscription because it commits the confessor to nothing specific, and that is contrary to the

meaning of confessional discourse. Now the *quatenus* formula could be turned to the present, committing us to the confessions only "insofar as" they are relevant to modern times. But that is also nonspecific and therefore confessionally vacuous.

4. A fourth type is that of anti-confessional biblicism. Earlier Lutherans steeped in pietistic biblicism and contemporary Lutherans locked into American Protestant neo-evangelicalism have no use for the confessions, but prefer to go right back to the Bible. Protestants who claim the right of private interpretation do not need to check their signals with the Catholic tradition; they get their signals directly from the Spirit. Paul Tillich often referred to "the leaping theory of Protestantism." Some Protestants leap over the tradition back to the Bible and find there the sweet music of their own subjective experiences. Certain aspects of the charismatic movement today show signs of such an anti-confessional biblicism.

5. A fifth type of approach is one we would propose as most adequate. Let us call it constructive confessional Lutheranism. There are hopeful signs that many Lutherans today have come out of their confessional ghetto, prepared to reenter the mainstream of the Catholic tradition along with other Christian communities in the ecumenical movement. Lutherans have not always been much concerned about the principle of continuity with the substance of the Catholic tradition. The Reformation movement petered out into various forms of Protestant sectarianism, Lutheranism being one of them. In addition to the principle of continuity, there is another aspect to the meaning of "constructive," and that is the principle of contemporaneity. The confessional principle is not constructive but, rather, destructive if it does not assist the church to preach the gospel and actualize its reality within every new situation in which it finds itself in mission. Each of the above manifestations of Lutheranism fails to incorporate either the principle of continuity or the principle of contemporaneity. The abandonment of either principle results in an abridged form of the church.

The purpose of the remainder of this chapter is to offer some viewpoints which might be helpful to guide us toward a new confessional orientation that does justice both to the classic witness of the church, without being archaistic, and to the present needs and insights of theology, without being faddistic. As Lutherans we must operate today in a kind of authority vacuum. There is simply no one voice in the church which can decide where we stand on matters of faith and morals. We do not have a magisterium in the present interim of a divided church. At dif-

ferent times in our Lutheran history we have been led now by the ruling
of the dogmaticians, now by the consensus of bureaucrats, now by a national parliament, and now by a democratic majority of clergy and laity,
mostly ill-prepared to grapple with the burning issues of the day. Where
do we go from here?

THE SELF-UNDERSTANDING
OF THE CONFESSIONS

Our own interpretation of the confessional principle in theology starts
with the self-understanding of the confessional writings themselves. We
would not wish to be in conflict with the sense in which the confessions
propose to address the church.

1. The confessions say very little about themselves. They are so overwhelmingly preoccupied with the act of confessing the gospel that they
very seldom reflect on the significance of what they are doing for later
times. They provide no formula of subscription for later generations of
Lutherans, and therefore seem to leave room for the possibility of adopt-
ing either a legalistic or an evangelical attitude toward creedal
statements.

2. The confessions always speak in the indicative rather than the imperative mood. They introduce many of their statements by saying: "We
believe, confess, and teach . . ." They do not declare what *must* be
believed in a law-oriented sense, but simply tell the world what they do
confess on the basis of faith in the gospel of Christ. They do not present
themselves as legal doctrine but as gospel witness, not as dogmas founded
on church authority but as testimonies of faith in accord with the scriptural record. If they are taken as legally binding canonical norms, they
may lose their value as witness to the gospel. It is a sad truth, of course,
that Lutherans have often dealt with their confessions in a legalistic
sense. That is symbololatry—a typically Lutheran form of idolatry.

3. The confessions always subordinate their witness to the Holy Scriptures of the Old and New Testaments. They distinguish between the Holy
Scriptures and all other religious classics by confessing that "Holy Scripture remains the only judge, rule, and norm according to which as the
only touchstone all doctrines should and must be understood and judged
as good or evil, right or wrong."[2] All other writings and symbols "are not
judges like Holy Scripture, but mere witnesses and expositions of the
faith, setting forth how at various times the Holy Scriptures were
understood in the church of God by contemporaries with reference to

controverted articles and how contrary teachings were rejected and condemned."[3] These assertions make clear that we do not place our Lutheran confessions above the Scriptures and that we cannot settle doctrinal disputes with proof texts from *The Book of Concord*, for the confessional writings themselves direct us to search the Scriptures. The church is fallible, church councils can err, and so also the Lutheran confessions may contain mistakes. Their claim to be faithful witnesses to the truth of the gospel and to be the summary content, rule, and standard by which all dogmas and teachings shall be tested is itself subject to testing by each succeeding generation of confessors. For the authority they claim for themselves is derived from their connection with the Scriptures and the gospel's authority.

When Lutherans say they are "bound to the confessions," they are using dangerously legalistic language that conveys the impression that we tilt more to the side of heteronomy and authoritarianism in matters of religion than to the side of autonomy and freedom. Lutherans invariably project a conservative image among the churches, as though they were addicted to things of the past such as the "good old days of orthodoxy." The confessional principle intends no such thing. We should rather witness positively to the power of the confessions to free us for genuine insight into the gospel. Creeds and confessions, in analogy with the Scriptures themselves, are truly capable of serving the church as "emancipation proclamations." We have only to be reminded of the function of the Barmen Declaration in the critical hour of the German church struggle against the heresy of the "German Christians." This sort of thing could happen because it hinged on the great confessional tradition of the Lutheran and Reformed traditions. Nonconfessional churches could provide no concerted defense against the Aryan heresy. The confessing church derived great strength and freedom from its ability to reassert its confession of the lordship of Christ against all usurpers and pretenders to the throne. Under persecution and attack, the Christians of the Confessing Church *(Bekennende Kirche)* experienced the liberating effects of being bound to a confession.

A confession lives in the church in terms of *kairos* and crisis. The church formulates a confession in a special *kairos* to face a particular crisis. The confessions are not like Bartlett's quotations or a set of timeless axioms. They breathe the air of their time. Therefore, we need not be anxious when we discover many sections in the confessional documents that seem totally irrelevant to our time and situation. It would be sophomoric to require that every confessional utterance be loaded with existential relevance for all times and places in the church's history. It is wholly erroneous to say that these confessions are not our confessions because we would not write them that way, or because we are not fully convinced about everything they say. That would be like saying one would not inherit one's father's house and live in it because modern architects do not design houses that way anymore. Each confessional statement may have its own hour in the total life of the people of God in history. What does not speak to us or for us today may become the source of guidance and renewal for others in a future hour of the church's life. The shape of a living confession in the church is always horizontal, bearing witness to the historicity of God's way with his people.

THE HERMENEUTICAL FUNCTION
OF THE CONFESSIONS

The Lutheran confessional heritage stands for a concrete and specific witness to the gospel, continuous with the Catholic dogmatic consensus and in response to a new set of questions posed at a particular time in church history. The Lutheran confessions speak on a vast variety of subjects, to be sure, but what they essentially constitute in addition to the classical dogmas is a new definition of the doctrine of justification by faith alone, undergirded by the christological presuppositions required to carry this burden and rounded off with the soteriological implications that exhibit its meaning.

The heart of the confessions—justification through faith alone apart from works—gives us the key to the right interpretation of the Scriptures. Is this hermeneutical key still relevant to our times? It is surely not a magic key to open all doors. It unlocks the door to the Scriptures insofar as the question of how things stand with us before God is concerned—insofar as we are dealing with the question of salvation, with all the bad news and good news that can truthfully be told about the human situation in light of God's revelation in Jesus Christ. If dogmaticians or exegetes do not use this hermeneutical key in biblical interpretation, they will inevitably use some other one. For there is simply no presuppositionless approach to the Scriptures. Scientific historians who imagine that the Scriptures can be studied without any presuppositions are simply not aware of the ones they implicitly bring to their research.

The confessions possess hermeneutical significance for us because they act like a signpost or compass. They point beyond themselves to the saving revelation in Christ and to the main events and authoritative interpretations of those events in the history of salvation. When Lutheran exegetes ask what the confessions can do for them in their exegetical tasks, the answer is that they provide them with a map for their exegetical explorations through the Scriptures. They are told that this map has been used before and has proved itself helpful to previous generations. They in turn are expected to check up on the map, to see if it conforms to their actual findings. Exegesis in the church is thus a two-way street. The narrow confessionalist is one who is satisfied to put the map in a pocket and forget about the trip. The anti-confessionalist is one who sets off on the trip without taking along a map, or takes one that has not been tested by others. The former sees the confessions as an end in themselves, whereas the latter fails to see them as a means to an end.

The question we face today as Lutherans is whether justification by faith alone is still the right key for the church. After all, the purpose of our confessional proposal is not to hold on to our own private key, but to serve the whole church and its witness to the gospel. Perhaps if the tiny word *sola* would be dropped, our Lutheran proposal would become ecumenically more palatable. Do we still mean to affirm the three *solas*—grace alone, faith alone, Christ alone? The entire significance of the Lutheran "dogmatic proposal"[4] lies in the meaning of the *solas*. This cannot be tolerated as a Lutheran peculiarity in the context of ecumenical pluralism, as one denominational dish in a world's fair of ecclesiastical specialties, along with papal authority, episcopal succession, presbyteral polity, congregational autonomy, liturgical formalism, orthodox mysticism, methodistic moralism, or charismatic spirituality. With the omission of the *solas* the gospel itself is betrayed, not only our Lutheran gospel, but the one and only gospel on which the one church and all its members are radically dependent. If the *raison d'être* of Lutheranism is not oriented to the ongoing reform of the *una sancta catholica et apostolica ecclesia* in terms of the article of justification by faith alone apart from the law, then Lutheranism has defaulted on the promise of its reforming mission. Then in establishing itself as an independent church alongside other churches, each left to its self-indulging ways, Lutheranism has indeed exchanged the true marks of the church for those of a sect.

There are two parallel movements in modern world Christianity. The one is a drive toward the revitalization of a particularistic confessional consciousness; the other is a rapprochement of church traditions toward the attainment of a universal Christian consciousness. As a rule these two movements are competitive. Rightly understood, however, Lutheran particularism exists not for its own sake but as a service of the whole church. The Lutheran thing is to challenge each particular community to search and find its own deep ground of faith in the Christ of the gospel. We are confident that as each tradition enters into the depths of its particular confessional consciousness to determine therein what truly possesses the status of ecumenical validity, there will be a meeting of minds in the gospel of Christ. And that is all we ask. Article VII of the Augsburg Confession says, "It is enough!" "For the true unity of the church it is enough (*satis est*) to agree concerning the teaching of the gospel and the administration of the sacraments." This should remind us that Lutherans best serve the interests of the ecumenical movement when they are true to the substance of their own confessions.

Lutherans make such a strong claim for the hermeneutical significance and systematic place of the justification principle that every generation is forced to make a critical reassessment. As for Luther himself, there could be no doubt: "As I often warn, therefore, the doctrine of justification must be learned diligently. For in it are included all the other doctrines of our faith; and if it is sound, all the others are sound as well."[5] In recent times Hans Iwand reaffirmed Luther's claim: "If we remove the article of justification from its central place, then we will be scarcely in a position any longer to know why we are and should remain evangelical Christians. Then we may as well surrender the purity of the gospel and settle instead for the unity of the church."[6]

Justification by faith alone would not be the article by which the church stands or falls if it were just one among many in a book of doctrines. Justification is that doctrine which controls the meaning of the whole and all its parts. Sad to say, justification lost its central hermeneutical standing in the post-Reformation periods of orthodoxy, Pietism, Enlightenment, and nineteenth-century Protestantism. Some of the current formulae were retained, as in Lutheran orthodoxy, but justification was treated as simply one of the many steps in the *ordo salutis*.[7] With the exception of Martin Kähler's work, justification never became the constructive principle of dogmatics, and its standing in contemporary Protestant theology is far from impressive, measured by the intent of our confessional heritage to use it as a tool in the decision for the true preaching of the gospel.

CHALLENGES TO OUR CONFESSIONAL PRINCIPLE

Our confessional boat seems to have sprung a leak at both ends—fore and aft. Hans Küng, speaking as a truly Catholic theologian, argued in his masterful work on Karl Barth's doctrine of justification that the doctrine of justification is *not* the central dogma of Christianity.[8] His point was that the Reformation doctrine of justification is only one doctrine within the fullness of Catholic tradition, just one bead on a string of doctrines clasped together by the unity of the church. But what guarantees the unity of the church? Since writing his book on justification, Hans Küng went on to question the Roman Catholic teaching on papal infallibility, which has traditionally worked as the guarantee of that unity. What alternative can he offer?

The Roman Catholic rejection of justification as the central datum of Scripture has been reinforced by many schools of biblical theology which view the Pauline doctrine of justification as a subsidiary theme, a "minor crater," as Albert Schweitzer said, not only in the New Testament as a whole, but also in the Pauline corpus of writings. This means that our confessional *sola fide* may be out of sync with our *sola scriptura*. The historical-exegetical base of the Lutheran doctrine of justification has crumbled even among some notable Lutheran biblical theologians. Some of these are claiming that not only is the theme of justification not central in Paul, but it has also suffered distortion by the allegedly "introspective conscience of the West" in the line from Augustine to Luther.

To a large extent the focus of both historical scholarship and theological interest has shifted from the "righteousness of God" in Paul's theology to the "kingdom of God" in Jesus' message. With respect to the starting point of Christology, we agree that we can no longer begin with Paul's teaching about justification by faith but must start with Jesus' preaching of the kingdom of God. We would want to argue, however, that it is a mistake to place justification and kingdom of God in opposition to each other. Paul's message of the righteousness of God was not at all discontinuous with Jesus' announcement of the coming rule of God. The justification of the sinner and the godless in Paul's theology communicates the righteousness of God, and that, for both Jesus and Paul, is exclusively a predicate of the power and dominion of God's oncoming kingdom. None can enter the kingdom of God except they come clothed with a righteousness not their own, but given from above. The righteousness that counts in the court of God's kingdom can only be received as a gift.

The idea of the kingdom of God was the chief theological category of the social gospel movement and is currently making a comeback in various liberation theologies. Both the older and newer theologies of the kingdom have shown a distinct tendency to operate with a synergistic paradigm of salvation. The right combination of divine grace and human praxis will work together to bring about the kingdom of God on earth. The critical metatheological function of the article of justification can help coordinate the construction of a new theology of the kingdom of God on a monergistic model.

The question we face as Lutherans today is whether we can still claim, in face of our current knowledge of Christian origins, that the message of justification is the true summary of the gospel we hear from Scripture. That is the challenge of our historical origins. But there is an equally strong challenge from our contemporary reading of the human situation. Our confessional position assumes that the message of justification touches the human condition at the point of its greatest need. What justification points to is supposed to embody the concern of every person, whether the farmer at the plow, the artisan in the shop, the scholar in the study, or the lawyer pleading a case in court. The need to which justification refers is existentially perennial and universal. Unfortunately, that is not commonly acknowledged to be the case in most schools of contemporary theology. If it is true that we have now entered an epoch which has evolved beyond the need for the central thrust of the Reformation, then the reason for the schism in the Western church may no longer be valid. Then the schism is nothing but tragic, for the clear assumption of our confessional posture is that the message of justification provides the right and true answer to the inescapable religious question of every person in every age and in every culture. It is not the intent of our confessions to immortalize the anxiety of just one sixteenth-century individual, Martin Luther, who was supposedly afflicted by an overactive introspective conscience.

Lutherans give the rest of the ecumenical world the impression of having had their confidence shaken upon entering the modern world. Who can forget the Helsinki fiasco of 1963 when Lutherans from around the world expressed serious doubt whether the message of justification was relevant any longer to the so-called "modern man"? This question of its relevance is as important as the biblical status of justification. The question of the standing or falling of the church is linked to the past source of the gospel as well as to the present situation in which the preaching of the Word takes place. At Helsinki, Lutherans issued a proclamation which stated: "The man of today no longer asks, 'How can I find a gracious God?' His question is more radical, more elementary: he asks about God as such, 'Where is God?' He suffers not from God's wrath, but from the impression of his absence; not from sin, but from the meaninglessness of his own existence; he asks not about a gracious God, but whether God really exists." Karl Barth seems to have anticipated this Lutheran farce when he wrote in his *Church Dogmatics* a decade before: "Of all the superficial catchwords of our age, surely one of the most superficial is that, whereas sixteenth-century man was concerned about the grace of God, modern man is much more radically concerned about God himself and as such."[10]

Is it really true that the question of the existence of God can be so clearly separated from the question of the grace of God, and is it really the deeper question? This is a question we cannot answer in this chapter, since here we are asking whether the originating claim of Lutheranism as a confessing movement for the sake of the church catholic is still the perpetuating dynamic of its identity. If what made us separate is no longer what keeps us separate, then we ought to realize that we are in the precarious situation of a sect.

My personal conviction is that the contemporary situation still calls for just such a radical and comprehensive doctrine of justification by faith alone as is defined by the confessions, that this is still an essential control-formula of dogmatics for the sake of the true and right proclamation of the gospel, and that this route is still our best ecumenical hope for realizing the unity of the church. What I am asserting seems to me to formulate an essential minimum condition of the theological legitimacy of continuing the Lutheran confessing movement. Anything less than this condemns the movement to the role of a sect unworthy of our support.

It is at least a workable hypothesis that our confessional identity is still in the position to meet the historical challenge of Christian *origins* as well as the contemporary challenge of *meaning,* and thus legitimate the ongoing mission of the Lutheran confessing movement for the sake of reforming the whole church by the criterion of justification—*sola gratia, sola fide, solus Christus.* This possibility could be documented by the works of numerous contemporary theologians—Barth, Bultmann, Gogarten, Ebeling, Käsemann, Stuhlmacher, Nygren, Aulén, Tillich, Iwand, Trillhaas, Dantine, and many others, including a current crop of American Lutheran theologians.

However, this working hypothesis may fail to meet the challenge of the future, whose forces could bury us all in the rubble of history. The chief creative efforts of Lutheran theologians have contributed to a positive correlation of Christianity with the modern world since the Enlightenment. Surely, from the time of the Enlightenment, Lutherans have done their most creative work in the closest relation to the developing culture of modernity. Although some Lutherans in Europe and

America have tried to ignore or deny that relation, shivering defensively in their confessionalistic ghettos, others have been in the vanguard of welcoming and accommodating the achievements of modern culture. However, there are many voices today prophesying the beginning of the end of the Enlightenment. What contribution our confessional heritage might make in the midst of our changing cultural world remains completely hidden. Some among the giants I mentioned above already have their names etched on tombstones; others have made plans for retirement. We are yet in the situation of presiding over the synthesis of Christianity and modernity that took its shape from the Enlightenment. This is why the philosophies of Kant and Hegel continue to exercise so much influence in present-day theology.

The whole system of Wolfhart Pannenberg may be remembered in future history as the closing of an era, not the opening of a new one. That system still moves, as we all do, within the basic horizons opened up by the Enlightenment, moving forward in turn from one new method of science to another, from *natural* science, to *historical* science, and last to *social* science. Pannenberg's most recent major work, *Theology and the Philosophy of Science*, charts the manner in which theology can establish the truth and the meaning of Christianity within the universe of modern science and scholarship. However, it is just this universe of meaning which may now be crumbling and along with it everything which is bound to its chances of survival. Christianity in the West is profoundly committed to the scientific, technological, industrial, and social dreams generated out of the post-Enlightenment era. This is most conspicuous in the evangelical groups that link their fundamentalist biblicism to the most advanced electronic techniques.

There are signs of disintegration of the cultural world that trusted in the competence of science and technological progress to guarantee that the world's people would ultimately enjoy an abundant supply of consumer goods. Many are now saying that the scientific form of consciousness is not the only one that puts us in touch with reality out there, that technology has progressed to the point of producing the means to destroy all civilization, that the consumer goods are being unevenly distributed between the haves and the have-nots, and that our liberal-democratic-capitalist system has proven itself as incapable of coping with this menacing problem as any of its rivals.

The question we face is whether our confessional tradition can be a beacon of hope when all around us the foundations of our post-Enlightenment culture seem to be shaking. There is no *mythos* or *logos* or *ethos* that seems to possess any power to grasp either the masses or the leaders of Western culture. The older, enthusiastic belief in providence or progress has yielded to a defensive mentality of hanging on and shoring up in face of our enemies. But who are the enemies? The tragedy is that we keep looking for the enemy aggressors out there whereas, in truth, our nemesis is being generated out of the very structures of science, technology, industrial development, rational thought, and autonomous freedom that we have explicitly trusted would in time build a more blessed universal culture. As in the biblical story of creation and fall, sin arises from within as the corruption of something good.

If we are heading into stormy weather, our cherished forms collapsing, our ideals and ideologies deeply suspect as masks covering our own self-interest, our very life threatened by the destruction of our natural environment and nuclear insanity, then what kind of confession can conceivably sustain us in such a cultural holocaust? What kind of a faith will be meaningful when the modes of existence we have been able to take for granted are beginning to vanish, when the eternal verities built into the nature of things no longer supply the meanings by which people live? We will then be plunged into a time when, stripped of all the "gods" of our Western culture, we will perhaps again need a "small catechism," one that speaks of a faith that is very much *sola*—all other systems of hope having failed us. Just such a test in the fire and judgment of God's history will prove whether our confessional heritage points to what is essential in biblical faith or stands merely as a monument to a Christian sectarian movement that lived in Northern Europe and North America during the second half of the second millennium A.D. Only such a test will purge away all the sectarian slag, extraneous to the pure metal of the gospel, which now stands in the way of the unity of the church. If Christianity will manage to survive the demise of our cultural epoch, it will be because the power of its own revealed truth will succeed in confirming itself in the midst of the turbulent transitions from this epoch to the next. Our confessional commitment entails a thrust toward the future, providing at least a particular point of departure for theology continuous with the meaning of the gospel of God's justification by which the church lives or dies. As the church moves into a new wilderness, however apocalyptic in kind, we have a compass to help us know something about our whereabouts and the direction in which we are going. There may be no maps yet to chart our way, but we will not be adrift without an orientation.

In view of the current challenges to the Lutheran confessional principle, it would seem that a genuine subscription to or acceptance of the confessional writings could hardly occur honestly without considerable mental reservation. However, before we jump to that conclusion, we ought to reflect on what it means to subscribe to any set of historic creeds and confessions in an evangelical manner. Minimally, a genuine subscription means that we affirm substantial correspondence between our witness to the gospel today and the content of the ecumenical creeds and confessional writings of the Reformation. This does not mean that we must write theology as Luther and Melanchthon did. Nor does it mean that we are able to vouch for every detail we care to inspect in the confessions. An acceptance of the confessions "without reservation" can at best mean agreement with the intention and meaning of the confessions, centering on the article of justification, and drawing out the essential corollaries of faith. In this sense we can accept the symbolical books of Lutheranism not only insofar as (*quatenus*) but also because (*quia*) they are the presentation and explanation of the pure doctrine of the gospel and a trustworthy summary of the faith of the Christian church. To subscribe to these confessions means to say "Here I stand!"

NOTES

1. Peter Brunner, "The LWF as an Ecclesiological Problem," *Lutheran World* 7, no. 3 (December 1960): 237-56.

2. Formula of Concord, Epitome, Comprehensive Summary 7, *The Book of Concord*, trans. and ed. Theodore G. Tappert (Philadelphia: Fortress Press, 1959), p. 465.

3. Ibid., Comprehensive Summary 8, p. 465.

4. I am indebted to Robert W. Jenson for this particular expression. Cf. Eric W. Gritsch and Robert W. Jenson, *Lutheranism: The Theological Movement and Its Confessional Writings* (Philadelphia: Fortress Press, 1976).

5. "Galatians Commentary (1535)" *LW* 26:283.

6. Hans Joachim Iwand, *Glaubensgerechtigkeit nach Luthers Lehre*, 3rd ed. (Munich: Kaiser Verlag, 1959), p. 6.

7. See my chapter, "The Correlation of Justification and Faith in Evangelical Dogmatics," *The New Community in Christ*, ed. James Burtness and John Kildahl (Minneapolis: Augsburg Publishing House, 1963), pp. 96-124.

8. Hans Küng, *Justification: The Doctrine of Karl Barth and a Catholic Reflection*, trans. Thomas Collins, Edmund E. Tolk, and David Granskou (New York: Thomas Nelson & Sons, 1964), pp. 6-11.

9. See Krister Stendahl, "The Apostle Paul and the Introspective Conscience of the West," *Harvard Theological Review* 56 (July 1963): 199-216.

10. Karl Barth, *Church Dogmatics*, ed. G. W. Bromiley and T. F. Torrance (Edinburgh: T. & T. Clark, 1956), 4:530.

3 The Ecumenical Principle

DEFINING THE CHURCH

The Reformation of Martin Luther was not the inauguration of a new church. The chief aim of Luther and of those who joined his movement was to reform the only church they knew—the Roman Catholic church. Luther and Melanchthon as well as all of the confessing fathers who built on their foundations saw themselves in accord with the consensus of the first five centuries, particularly as this was expressed in the creeds and councils of the ancient church. The abuses in the church were attacked as medieval innovations which stood condemned by the Word of God, even though they had the backing of the bishops and popes in that period. At the center of the Reformation movement was the proposition that the church and all its attributes of unity, holiness, catholicity, and apostolicity derived radically from the gospel of Jesus Christ as Lord and Savior, as the foundation of the church and its reason for being.

Article VII of the Augsburg Confession states: "For the true unity of the church it is enough to agree concerning the teaching of the gospel and the administration of the sacraments." In this same article, the only definition of the church we find is this: "The church is the assembly of saints in which the gospel is taught purely and the sacraments are administered rightly."

The church, however, never appears in history in a pure form. Luther retained Augustine's distinction between the visible and the invisible church. The visible church is a *corpus mixtum,* and the line between believers and unbelievers is invisible and therefore cannot be drawn by us on this side of the day of judgment. The true church is always an object of faith, not subject to empirical verification as though the "true" believers could be identified by the right kind of test. We believe the church is truly present where the power of the Holy Spirit is at work through the Word and Sacraments. These are the means by which Christ becomes present and therefore the signs by which we can tell whether a particular gathering of people is really the church.

The Lutheran tradition, following Luther, has stressed the notion of the universal priesthood of all believers, mediated through baptism. "Whoever comes out of the water of baptism can boast that he is already a consecrated priest, bishop, and pope."[1] But this does not mean that just anyone can step forth into the office of the ministry of Word and Sacraments. That would lead to anarchy.

> Because we are all priests of equal standing, no one should push himself forward and take it upon himself, without our consent and election, to do that for which we all have equal authority. For no one dare take upon himself what is common to all without the authority and consent of the community.[2]

These two poles, universal priesthood and ordained ministry, have survived in the Lutheran tradition to this day so that it is not difficult to tell the difference between clergy and laity in Lutheran congregations.

The theological formulation of the essential difference between clergy and laity continues to be an area of controversy in Lutheran theology. The poles of controversy may be characterized in terms of the tension between the Protestant principle and Catholic substance, to use Tillich's language. The Protestant pole stresses the universal priesthood of all believers. Who then is the minister? The minister is one who has been delegated by this group to perform certain functions in behalf of all. This is also called the transferal theory of the ministry. When the ministry is derived from the congregation, the minister is seen as a delegated representative of the people, assuming functions that belong to all the people so that things may be done "decently and in order." Here the authority of the ministry is derived "from below." The other pole sees the special ministry as set apart by dominical institution, which has been passed on by a succession of officeholders and symbolized by the laying on of hands. Here the authority of the ministry is derived from above.

Luther can be quoted on both sides of the controversy. He could argue that we need ministers for practical reasons: What would happen if everyone wanted to speak? It would result in chaos, Luther said, like the chatter of housewives on their way to market, all talking at once and nobody listening. Likewise, if many hands were doing baptism, the poor baby would drown. But Luther also said: "I say (that) according to the institution of Christ and the apostles, every city should have a priest or bishop, as Paul clearly says in Titus 1."[3]

To some extent this controversy lies behind the so-called "high church" and "low church" trends in Lutheranism, past and present. However, many of the distinctions between these two trends are cosmetic. They fall in the category of the "adiaphora." Whatever the theory—high, low, or

in between—Lutherans have generally shared a consensus on the following points: (1) a rejection of the Roman Catholic view of ordination as
conferring an indelible character on a special priestly class;[4] and (2) the
need for an official ministry of the church properly called, for the public
proclamation of the Word and the administration of the sacraments.

If, compared with other major groups, Lutherans appear to have waf-
fled on the doctrine of the ministry, it is well to remember that
Lutheranism was a movement that emerged in a situation of crisis in
church history. On the one side, Lutherans were fighting against the
errors of Rome and had to improvise some kind of church order to continue the ministry once they lost the support of the duly constituted
episcopacy. On the other side, Lutherans were frightened by the extreme
of the "spiritualists," who based their ministries on a direct inner call of
the Spirit. Luther and his followers did not expect to see the emergency
situation develop into a state of normalcy. Many efforts were made, and
many Lutherans are now renewing the effort, to restore something lost
during the sixteenth-century schism. The dialogues between Lutherans
and Roman Catholics must be seen as steps on the way to a healing of the
breach.

The emphasis on gospel and sacraments as the essence of the church
has kept Lutherans free for a variety of church structures. In ecumenical
discussions Lutherans have characteristically accented faith and true doctrine rather than polity and church order. As a result Lutherans have
been able to enter into many different types of relationship with the state
and society. Calvinists, by contrast, have shown a greater desire to enlist
the power of the state to carry out the will of God in political and
cultural life. The "social gospel" earlier in this century and the "Moral
Majority" today are both the products of Calvinist activism. Lutherans,
by comparison, look like a bunch of "quietists."

One of our traditional slogans has been: *ecclesia semper reformanda*.
In keeping with this, many Lutherans today have renewed the original
self-understanding of Lutheranism as a confessing movement for the sake
of the church catholic.[5] The prime purpose of the Lutheran movement is
to continue the liberation process which Luther began. The church was in
bondage to Rome. Liberation would mean removing three walls which
the Roman church had built in its defense: (1) the superiority of the pope,
bishops, priests, and monks over the laity; (2) the exclusive right of the
pope to interpret Scripture authoritatively; and (3) the claim that only
the pope could summon a council and confirm its acts.[6] In his *Babylonian
Captivity of the Church*, Luther pointed again to three items from which
the church suffered: (1) the denial of the place of the laity; (2) the doc-

trine of transubstantiation; and (3) the teaching that the mass is a good work and a sacrifice. As these walls come tumbling down, the reasons for Lutherans to continue their protest movement against the *Romanization* of the church catholic would seem to be greatly diminished.

Twenty years ago I spoke to Lutheran pastors of the Illinois Synod of the Lutheran Church in America, calling for the reunion of separated Christians in one catholic church.[7] I used a parable likening Protestants to exiles.[8] Exiles do hope to return to their homeland; exiles do dream of reunion with their fellow countrymen. But they know this is impossible under the present regime. Meanwhile, they live in protest and fight for a change in government back home. However, sometimes they become smug and self-sufficient and convert their interim status into a permanent establishment. That is the fate of Protestantism.

Different versions of this address were published. The Religious News Service reported that a Lutheran theologian in Chicago had called for a Protestant "return to Rome." A *Christian Century* editorial was entitled "Protestant Hara-Kiri," dubbing my proposal "absurd," "mischievous," "odious," and "dangerous." If the same address and articles were reissued today, they would hardly cause a ripple. Times have changed. The official Lutheran-Catholic dialogues have reached the same conclusion that I was advancing: the Lutheran protest centers on the freedom to proclaim the Word and share the sacraments according to the scriptural witness to evangelical truth. This protest does not rule out the papal and episcopal structures in the church, but only those dogmas and authoritarian practices out of sync with the gospel. Church structures must always be radically in the service of gospel truth.

Some of us have said it so often that it hardly bears repeating: Lutheranism is not essentially a church but a movement. It is not essentially an independent church in competition with other denominational churches. It is a confessional movement that exists for the sake of reforming the whole church of Christ by the canon of the gospel. The ecclesiastical, organizational structures of Lutheranism are interim measures, ready to go out of business as soon as their provisional aims are realized.

THE SIGNIFICANCE OF
THE ECUMENICAL MOVEMENT

The twentieth century has been called the "age of the church," and the ecumenical movement is the most striking evidence supporting this assessment. The twentieth century has also witnessed the reaffirmation of the role of eschatology in systematic theology. There is today a new interpretation of the biblical concept of the kingdom of God that binds the doctrine of the church to eschatology. This eschatological perspective is the leitmotif of our revision of the fundamental principles of Lutheran theology. When eschatology and ecclesiology break apart into separate complexes, serious distortions arise in the life of the church and its theology which can keep the various Christian communities off the path that leads to the recovery of unity. The goal of more faithfully embodying the attributes of the true church of Jesus Christ is made more distant. In the Nicene-Constantinopolitan Creed, we confess that we believe in the "one holy, catholic, and apostolic church." But there are eschatologically motivated movements in worldwide Christianity that drive to the future of the kingdom of God without seeking any present embodiment of that future in the life of the church in history. Individual believers zoom off into the clouds of an otherwordly future, leaving the institutional church behind in the grip of the dragon and the beast of a fallen history. America has been the scene of numerous eschatological sects without much sense of the church. There are millions of such believers who have nothing whatsoever to do with the ecumenical movement.

At the other extreme are the various mainline branches of Christianity strongly influenced by a tradition, reaching back to Augustine and permeating the Constantinian order, that virtually equates the church with the kingdom of God. This is a legacy still deeply entrenched in our church praxis, although in theory it has lost all support. This absorption of eschatology into ecclesiology—we can call it the de-eschatologizing of Christianity—contributed to the various kinds of ecclesiocentricity that have expressed themselves at every level of the church's life: its doctrine, worship, preaching, evangelism, stewardship, mission policy, and institutional politics. The kingdom of God is so fully realized in the past that the church has only to live from precedent, not truly open to the needs of the present or the challenges of the future.

There are certainly nontheological factors that partly account for the current ecumenical impasse. Here we are putting our finger on a theological factor, the role of eschatology in helping or hindering the churches to find their way to the goal of the ecumenical movement. This "age of the church" will end in dismal failure if the ecumenical movement does not succeed in breaking out of its current impasse and drawing the churches into a new kind of universal council. It is not utopian to believe that churches could overcome their own administrative church-centeredness to express the reality of the one church—in conciliar fellowship at the global level and in eucharistic communion at the local level.

Many people seem to have abandoned their enthusiasm for the ecumenical movement and its prospect of Christian unity in exchange for involvement in the social and political life of the world, which seems so much more relevant. I do not believe, however, that the ecumenical drive to reunite the churches in the common faith is an intramural affair, lacking in relevance for the social order. The relative social and political impotence of the churches is deeply rooted in the doctrinal controversies of the sixteenth century, which disrupted the unity of the medieval order. The rise of secularism in modern culture, the neutrality of the state in matters of religion, and the tendency to make faith a purely private thing are conditions which arose and still continue because the fragmentation of the church drives society to base its meaning and purpose on other than religious foundations. The religious wars in Europe and the ensuing denominational conflicts convinced people that religion must be excluded from the public realm and that religion, after all, is purely a private matter. Thus, when the churches attempt to speak out on political and social issues, as mutually antagonistic denominations they only succeed in canceling each other out, thus depriving the public realm of its religiously and morally based motivations and judgments. When leaders of one denomination speak out, the public at large becomes suspicious that they are disguising the special interests of their own group in moral rhetoric or are guilty of meddling in public affairs, which is presumably none of their business as religious leaders. As the public realm becomes more and more neutral in moral and religious matters, a secular vacuum is created into which a host of new demons is bound to enter on a holiday, with the churches ill-equipped by virtue of their divisions to exercise the prophetic role of their own eschatological faith.

This is perhaps enough to show that the ecumenical movement is not merely an intra-ecclesiastical preoccupation. Christianity will not again become a meaningful social force, checking the excesses of the ruling *isms*, until it overcomes the denominational conflicts of the past and constructs new forms in which its own vision of life can once again become a resource for the common good. The ecumenical movement for Christian unity does not exist for its own sake, but for the good of the world. "That they may all be one . . . that the world may believe" (John 17:21).

The reconstructed unity of the church does not mean that the church will aim to restore the authoritarian structures of medieval Christendom which claimed to exercise the lordship of God over the state and over all believers; it may well be that a reunited church will never be more than a creative minority in a pluralistic culture. Yet it remains true that it can fulfill its mission in the world only under the condition of constructing a form of unity true to its essential nature as the one embodiment of Christ in history.

Since the splitting up of the unity of the church, we are confronted by a multiplicity of churches and sects, each of which claims to be an authentic representation of the true church of Jesus Christ. Each church claims to exist in continuity with the essence of the church and to embody all the essentials of the true church. No church has ever advertised itself as a false church or a pseudo-church. Sometimes its claims are advanced in exclusive terms, and all others are anathematized to the degree they differ on essentials. There has never been one church in history without rivals. As the church defined orthodoxy, heretics and schismatics continued to insist they were the true successors of the original church of the apostles. When the Western church broke up in the sixteenth century, the many Protestant groups were pressed to legitimate themselves in face of each other and of the Roman Catholic church by an appeal to primitive Christianity, and sometimes to the consensus of the first five centuries (*consensus quinquesaecularis*). This need to defend their claims with respect to Christian origins was a chief impetus in the rise of the critical-historical method.

But if the claims can be defended by the historical method, they can also in principle be overturned by the same method. And that is precisely what has happened. The claims of each and every church to be the legitimate successor of the apostolic church, to the exclusion of others, have been eroded by the acids of historical consciousness. Now such claims are maintained only where the historical method itself is ruled out, and these claims enjoy no credibility beyond their own circles. As Ernst Käsemann has shown in his famous article, "The Canon of the New Testament and the Unity of the Church,"[9] every church discovers in Scripture its own foundations, and that is because Scripture itself contains a multiplicity of confessions. The question of what and where the true church is has been radicalized by historical probings of Christian origins and the claim of every church to embody the fullness of the church is no longer credible even to its most loyal members.

The doctrine of the marks of the church emerged in a context of dispute, particularly in relation to Gnosticism, to provide criteria by which to tell whether the church is true or false. There are four such classical attributes: unity, holiness, catholicity, and apostolicity. These are not, however, self-evident descriptions of the empirical church. These criteria, which the anti-Gnostic fathers defined to tell the difference between the true and the false church, are themselves subject to controversy. What do they mean? Every sect has managed to affirm these attributes as self-designations, in the face of the most conspicuous contradiction, by transferring their meaning to an invisible realm to which it is related by an invisible faith. When these qualities become utterly invisible, they of course lose their value as criteria to discern the true church.

When the Reformers lifted up preaching the Word and administering the sacraments as essentials of the church, they did not thereby reject the four classical attributes, but they were pointing to the conditions without which the church could not exist at all. In the present ecumenical quest for the reality and fullness of the church, the two Reformation marks— Word and sacraments—and the four traditional attributes—unity, holiness, catholicity, and apostolicity—are clearly acknowledged by all churches as essential. A church that claims to be one, holy, catholic, and apostolic also claims to be founded on the true preaching of the Word and the right administration of the sacraments, and vice versa. Roman Catholics, Eastern Orthodox, and Protestants of all types make the same verbal claims, but they understand, embody, and practice these claims often in mutually contradictory ways. Churches will reach a new understanding in ecumenical dialogue as they fire these ecclesial attributes with new meanings and thus drive them beyond the current impasse into a new form of the church.

THE APOSTOLICITY OF THE CHURCH

I am going to deal with the attributes of the church in reverse order, beginning with the apostolic character of the church. The reason is that we can overcome the present divisions of the church only with reference to a common unifying past that lies deeper than them all. All churches have equal access to the apostolic period and claim to be grounded in primitive Christianity. There is power in our common apostolic source to overcome separations. We need to discover our common Christian identity in some kind of apostolic reality. No church can call itself Christian if it fails to preserve historical continuity with the apostolic origins of Christianity. The controversy between churches must in some way hinge on the question of what is authentically apostolic. So what is apostolic?

Apostolicity cannot be the norm of later church history and of present-day Christianity in the sense of demanding the repristination of the church of the apostolic period. Nor can apostolicity be used to discredit all later developments in church tradition. Moreover, historical research has wiped out the romantic picture of apostolic times as the golden age of the church, extending perhaps into the patristic era. The fall of the church, or the shadowy side of Christianity, can be tracked back to Judas and Peter and James and Paul and all the others. It seems clear that we cannot solve our difficulties by an archaistic return to apostolic times.

And yet we must retain continuity with what is apostolic. How is it possible to go back to what is essentially apostolic without getting stuck in the past or trying in vain to repeat it? The answer is that there is an *eschatological dynamic* at the heart of the apostolic witness that drives beyond the time-bound conditions of the apostolic age. This is the core of the New Testament gospel. This gospel possesses meaning for all later generations of believers by engaging them in a common mission and orienting them to a common future which that eschatological dynamic in their common apostolic past opens up. Continuity with the apostles does not mean constructing an irreducible minimum of apostolic doctrines, nor does it mean connecting up with an unbroken chain of apostolic offices of leadership, but it does mean to lay hold of the *original eschatological drive of the early Christian apostolate* and to trace its trajectory through the discontinuities of time and history.

It is commonly acknowledged that primitive Christianity was stamped by an eschatological consciousness, living in the presence of the absolute future which has already arrived in the person of Jesus Christ. The community of Christ already has a share of the final eschatological fulfillment through faith in Christ and presses on in hope toward a future consummation to which all peoples and things are moving. This eschatological consciousness was the compelling drive of the primitive Christian apostolate and must be the point of contact for every later attempt to define and retrieve what is essential in the concept of apostolicity. The core of this concept is the reappearance of the crucified Jesus—an event which the earliest witnesses interpreted as a resurrection occurrence within the framework of Jewish eschatological expectation. The immediate effect of the resurrection appearances of Jesus was to create a circle of apostles commissioned to preach the message of the power and presence of God's approaching kingdom in Jesus himself. The office of the apostle is centered in his witness to the resurrection of Jesus as God's proof that the coming of his kingdom is indissolubly linked to the personal life and ministry of Jesus. The apostolic mission is not only a reflection of the light of God's eschatological action in Jesus Christ, but it is also an instrument bearing God's universal promises to the nations. The eschatological meaning of Jesus is carried forward in the universal mission of the apostles.

At what point in history did the church lose the original eschatological dynamic of its apostolic origins? In point of fact the church did not lose it, but found new ways to formulate the decisive meaning of its apostolic foundations in subsequent historical situations. Thus, very early (second century) the church made a canon of apostolic writings, and later theology formulated the principle of *sola scriptura*. The New Testament appendix to the Hebrew Scriptures is a sign of the uniqueness of the apostolic period by virtue of its proximity to the decisive eschatological message preached by the apostles, by which all later generations of Christians must get their bearings in history because their share in that message determines the meaning and goal of their calling and mission. A church is apostolic by doing the apostolic thing. The eschatological message and the apostolic mission define the being and meaning of the church in history.

Centuries later the church formulated the trinitarian and christological dogmas. At first sight we are in the realm of Hellenistic philosophical categories. Actually, however, the church was expressing in the dogma of the incarnation—including the divinity of Christ and the hypostatic union of the divine and human natures—the unique, unsurpassable, and decisive appearance of eschatological salvation in Jesus Christ. Similarly, the Reformation doctrine of justification, renewing Augustine's fight against Pelagianism—*sola gratia, sola fides, solus Christus*—aims to frame the apostolic motif of God's decisive eschatological intervention in Christ for the world's salvation against every kind of moral and religious synergism which robs Christ of his honor. To be sure, orthodox Christianity frequently lost sight of the eschatological dynamic in the meaning of apostolicity and instead tried legalistically to repeat all the historically conditioned forms in which the apostolic mission expressed itself from age to age. The identification of apostolicity with past forms of orthodoxy accounts for the unhistorical way in which both Scripture and dogma have been interpreted in Roman Catholic and conservative Protestant traditions. What we need is a concept of apostolicity which can freely acknowledge the historical difference between the apostolic period and our present situation without severing the vein of truth that connects the church of today with the apostolic mission. The criterion of what is apostolic in the church's life—doctrine, worship, structure, and mission—is whatever means it takes to set forth the finality of truth and universality of meaning of that messianic salvation which promises to enlighten and transform the world. The canon, the cult, the creed, and the offices of the historic church can therefore be called apostolic not because such things are carbon copies of what can be found in the time of the apostles, but rather because they point to the comprehensive and liberating truth of the kingdom of God in Jesus and his resurrection from the dead. This eschatological concept of the apostolate opens the church to take seriously its own historicity, the special needs and opportunities of every new time and place, without having to carry along the outdated forms of the past. Things that were apostolic in earlier centuries may be irrelevant today, and things that were not perceived as apostolic not so long ago, such as the abolition of slavery and women's ordination, can be seen today as driven by the apostolic mission. What counts is not that the church replicate the past, but become free to be apostolic for its own time, often in contrast to the way of being apostolic in former times.

If we apply this eschatological concept of apostolicity to the ecumenical dialogues, we might be able to soften the differences between the confessions. Roman Catholics should be able to acknowledge the point of the *sola scriptura* principle of the Protestant Reformation, in the sense of Luther's radical hermeneutical principle of *was Christum treibt*, which makes the preaching of Christ according to the Scripture the criterion of apostolicity. And Protestants should be able to see that the point of the ecclesiastical offices—priesthood, episcopacy, and papacy—in the Catholic tradition is to continue the apostolic mission to the ends of the world and to the end of time, thus making the ordering of the church a derived criterion of apostolicity which Protestants need not refuse. Their teaching authority exists to interpret Scripture and the Christian faith in the succession of the apostles, and their success in doing this must be judged by the criterion of apostolicity, and cannot be guaranteed by the sheer fact of episcopal ordination. These two stresses—evangelical proclamation from the Protestant side and episcopal leadership from the Catholic side—are tasks that belong to apostolic succession by virtue of continuing the apostolic mission in the world, thus satisfying the requirements of the original eschatological character of the criterion of apostolicity. This criterion should make room for a great deal of flexibility in structuring offices and means of proclamation appropriate to new and changing historical situations as long as the aims and goals are defended by their relation to the eschatological nature of the apostolic mission.

THE CATHOLICITY OF THE CHURCH

By the catholicity of the church we have in mind the universal scope of the apostolic mission. The mission is universal because of its eschatological character. Therefore, a church can only be apostolic if it is also catholic, working in line with the universal horizon of the apostolic commission. In many Protestant circles the word "catholic" in the Nicene Creed was dropped in favor of the word "Christian." But this was a bad move because the word "Christian" is more suitably an equivalent for the world "apostolic," concentrating on the identity principle of the church. The word "catholic" has now been restored to the Creed for common liturgical use, and this can give rise to the salutary quest for authentic catholicity so conspicuous by its absence in many churches.

It was Ignatius of Antioch who said, "Where Jesus Christ is, there is the catholic church." "Catholic" means going beyond the limits of particularity, and for the church that calls for openness in two directions: to the eschatological future of God's kingdom and to the whole world in all its splendid diversity. Being entirely related to Christ, the church must be related to the universal reality beyond its own limits because the eschatological salvation that appeared in Christ embraces the meaning and future of the whole world and sends the church on its universal mission to carry the message of salvation to all people.

The essence of catholicity lies in the church's apostolic concern for the whole world. This means that catholicity includes not only the catholic heritage of past generations and the whole of present-day Christianity, but all generations to come. Only in the final glory of eschatological fulfillment will all the dimensions of catholic fullness be revealed. Catholicity is an eschatological concept, because the fullness of life and truth to which it refers is not yet realized in the concrete forms of the church along the way. Catholicity is not an empirical concept which describes the church as such; as an eschatological concept it points to the movement of the church's universal mission "to the ends of the earth" and "to the close of the age." Then Christ will hand his kingdom over to the Father and God will be all in all.

This eschatological catholicity should warn the church in history against demanding uniformity in any of its concrete forms of life, liturgy, and leadership. A church calls itself catholic despite the fact that its particular forms are only partial and provisional embodiments of catholic fullness. A church will manifest the catholic spirit not by equating itself with catholic fullness, but by holding itself open to the whole of the Christian tradition and by aiming at the universal goal of the apostolic mission.

Such an eschatological catholicity of apostolic depth and missionary breadth should foster a new appreciation of pluralism. The church should exist ahead of the world as the bearer of signs and promises that reach out to encompass the totality of reality on the way to its future destiny. If the church is to function in behalf of the kingdom of God for the world, it will be open to new things that happen on the frontline of history. That is the source of pluralism. Pluralism is of the essence of a church that functions on the borderline of the new and the old, that is open in all directions spatially and temporally. In its pioneering role the church will explore and experiment with cultural forms of expression beyond its existing fellowship, to see what can be integrated into its life as a sacrament of the multidimensional unity of humanity in the kingdom of God. The church catholic will affirm various forms of psychological and sociological life; it will affirm the various conditions of life that have to do with sex and age and race and language and culture and nationality, inviting all things to a rendezvous in the eschatological *pleroma* of God's kingdom.

If the catholic church takes its own eschatological relativity seriously, it will not triumphalistically turn in upon itself, absolutizing a sacred sphere, a sacred style, a sacred theology, a sacred language, a sacred liturgy—measuring proximity to the kingdom of God by the degree to which it cherishes the consecrated forms of its own tradition.

In the realm of doctrine we can no longer expect a tightly defined *consensus doctrinae* in which our denominations have lived in their separate ghettos. Now every confessional group is penetrated by a multiplicity of beliefs on every basic doctrine. This is due partly to the ecumenical dialogues, partly to a broader grasp of the classical tradition, and partly to a new openness to the secular world and other religions. The statement of Vincent of Lerins that catholic doctrine is that which is believed "everywhere, always, and by everyone" sounds strange in face of contemporary doctrinal pluralism. There is not a single doctrine about which that can be said now. Moreover this neglects the difference between the provisional historical and the final eschatological forms of truth. Truth is never static, and the fullness of truth is something Christians can only await from the eschatological future; for now we see only in fragmentary ways, even with respect to our clearest doctrinal formulations. In light of this eschatological idea of catholicity, should it not be possible for our different confessional traditions to see things in a new light and perhaps overcome past contradictions on the way to a new understanding of Christian truth? In order for truth to remain identical with itself, it must express itself under the conditions of changing historical forms. Roman Catholics have in principle acknowledged this point by means of the idea of the development of dogma, and Protestants have done so by relativizing church dogmas by the criterion of the apostolic gospel. The intentions of both sides can be unified by an eschatologically oriented concept of catholic truth.

THE HOLINESS OF THE CHURCH

The church is elected to be the holy people of God. This mark of the church, like the others, is not an empirical designation of a condition which anyone can see by observing the sanctimonious piety of its members. The holiness of the church is positional, not possessional; it is based on divine election. In the biblical and Christian tradition the doctrine of election has been a tangle of confusing ideas and a topic of controversial theology. In the official line from Augustine through Thomas Aquinas and Calvin, the doctrine of election became a matter of the predestination of individuals for their salvation, and this all happened in an eternal forum with little reference to history. Along this line the holiness of the church refers to the sum total of saints who have been chosen in a timeless eternity, selected one by one for no reason at all and destined for an otherworldly salvation as the aim of divine election. There is another line which begins to stand out in the light of history and eschatology.

We find the roots of a history-oriented doctrine of election in the Old Testament where Moses says to the people of Israel: "For you are a people holy to the Lord your God; the Lord your God has chosen you to be a people for his own possession, out of all the peoples that are on the face of the earth. It was not because you were more in number than any other people that the Lord set his love upon you and chose you, for you were the fewest of all peoples; but it is because the Lord loves you, and is keeping the oath which he swore to your fathers, that the Lord has brought you out with a mighty hand, and redeemed you from the house of bondage, from the hand of Pharaoh king of Egypt" (Deut. 7:6–8). The oath which the Lord swore to the fathers refers back to the call of Abraham where the goal of God's election is not simply Abraham and his posterity, but through Abraham to "all the families of the earth" (Gen. 12:3). Election means the selection of one for the sake of the many—not the election of saints for their eternal blessedness, but election for a mission with a universal goal, running from the Exodus to the *eschaton*. The chosen people are set apart for a purpose that does not end with Israel or the church but is related to the most comprehensive horizon of God's love for all humanity.

The holiness of the church is thus based on its chosenness for a mission of service to God's greater purpose in the world. The content of this holiness is not internal to the church's own sanctification, but is related to the struggles of God in the world, that "he will bring forth justice to the nations." (Isa. 42:1). The election of the holy people is for the mission of God in the context of the struggles now going on in world history. Election to the status of holiness is not for the church's eternal security, but for the continuation of God's historic mission to all the nations.

The holy church, the *communio sanctorum* set apart for mission, is still a fellowship of sinners, a *communio peccatorum.* This community never lives a single day in which it does not have to begin its mission again from scratch with the forgiveness of sins. The holy church is always *ecclesia reformata et semper reformanda,* and the agenda of things to be reformed is supplied not only by the imperfect church but by the goal of the church's mission to sanctify the whole world in the context of God's coming kingdom. If only the church and Christian people could be freed from anxiety about their own intrinsic holiness and view it instead under the sign of the cross in the struggles of God against the powers of evil in the world until the final establishment of the kingdom, we would not have here a mark which divides the church. For no church would have anything to boast about in face of others; no church is yet beyond the point of God's struggle for the increase of justice in social, economic, and political terms. Accepting the role of advocacy for the increase of peace and justice in the world is an intrinsic element of the mark of holiness that belongs to a church God has elected for a worldwide mission.

THE UNITY OF THE CHURCH

In the dogmatic constitution on the church of Vatican II, *Lumen Gentium,* the church is defined as a kind of *sacrament* and *instrument* of the unity of all humanity. In this constitution the eschatological horizon of the New Testament is integrated into the chapters on "The Mystery of the Church" (Chapter 1) and "The People of God" (Chapter 2), but is not carried through in the chapter on "The Hierarchical Nature of the Church" (Chapter 3). It states: "The mystery of the holy Church is manifest in her very foundation, for the Lord Jesus inaugurated her by preaching the good news, that is, the coming of God's kingdom." These initiatives of Vatican II are significant for the ecumenical efforts to recover the oneness of the church. Seeing the church as a sacrament of union with Christ and an instrument for promoting unity in the world should make it clear that the chief task of the churches today is to overcome the oppositions that divide them. It is a grotesque sight to see how Western Christianity has exported its dissensions to other lands and stamped the new churches with the names of its own peculiar brands.

The ecumenical search for the oneness of the church has reinforced the christocentric impulse of the classical Reformation tradition and of the neo-Reformation trends in twentieth-century theology. The way to the reunion of the churches goes through Jesus Christ. The counter-christological revolution in some recent theological works must be viewed as a threat to the health of the ecumenical movement. For it is Christ and Christ alone who is the unity of all Christians, the common focus of their faith and their common ground in the Word and Sacraments, no matter how many arguments Christians may have about important matters of doctrine and practice. So the unity of Christians in Christ is a *given* prior to anything that the ecumenical movement can do. Paradoxically, whatever the ecumenical movement should do can have no other kind of unity in mind than that which *already* exists among Christians in the communion to which they confess they belong in the words of the Nicene Creed —the one holy, catholic, and apostolic church. For they can realize their unity among themselves only as they meet each other as members of the one and same body in Christ.

That is just where a lot of Christians would like to leave the matter. The unity that counts is spiritual; it already exists through each person's faith in Christ. Nothing can or need be added to it. Hence there is no need for the ecumenical movement, which allegedly is only out to promote organizational union from the top down, producing a super-church of bureaucratic powers that looks very much like the fallen church of the Antichrist. What is wrong with this position, so common among conservative evangelicals? What is wrong may be called "ecclesiological docetism," making the unity of Christians a purely invisible one as if the divisions between Christians were not a sin against the unity grounded in Christ. What is wrong is the refusal to manifest in a visible way the invisible unity of the faith of all Christians at any one time and place. The Reformers intended to reform the one church, not to smash its unity into innumerable sects whose unity remains totally hidden. The sectarian pluralism of Protestantism is a sign of the failure of the Reformation, not of its success.

If the unity of the church is to become visible for the sake of the church's sacramental and instrumental relation to the world, there are two foci in which this must happen: Eucharist and ministry. The Eucharist is meant to be a source and sign of the universal unity among Christians. Instead, it has become the place where the most glaring denominational conflicts are mirrored. The proof that a hidden spiritual unity among Christians is not enough can be seen at the celebration of every Lord's Supper, for there a clear line is drawn between those who are welcome into the fellowship and those who are excommunicated. Every church shares in the guilt of these mutual excommunications.

The eschatological perspective on Eucharist should make it clear that this is not the church's supper to which it can issue an invitation to a closed meeting of members in good standing. A Eucharist that is denominationally limited to people who meet the requirements of church membership scarcely resembles a meal whose host is the One who practiced table fellowship with tax collectors and sinners. The boundaries of the Lord's Supper must be open as a sign of the openness of the messianic feast to which all the nations are invited. The risen Christ can walk through the walls that the churches have erected around their mealtimes. Such walls appear paper thin in light of the Christ who has torn down the dividing wall of hostility to make all people in the end one universal family in God.

Now the Eucharist is a proleptic foretaste of the coming kingdom. Now the Eucharist is a sign and sacrament of the eschatological eucharist —the feast of the nations. Now the Lord's Supper is sharing a meal with all those who want to eat and drink together in the fellowship of Christ. Now is the time for the churches to unite in the presence of the One who is to come, and who even now does come in the bread and the wine as the symbols of the great eschatological shalom. The glory of this eschatological unity must be allowed to glow sacramentally and symbolically at every local administration of the Eucharist. That is not now happening; yet that is the minimum of visibility which the mark of unity demands of our ecumenical work.

It is for the sake of the eschatological history of Christ in this eucharistic unity that the church as a whole has particular offices that specialize in giving expression to it. This ministry of unity is needed at every level: the local, the regional, the national, and the global. Without such an office or offices of special ministry, the unity of Christians cannot be visibly realized, and therewith the mission of the community of Christ to be a sacrament and servant of the unity of humanity is crippled. These serving offices must not become the tools of hierarchical bullies to lord it over the people. There is always the danger of transferring divine lordship to human lordship, but in Christ the meaning of lordship has been transformed into *diakonia*, and so must it be with all the offices of ministry in the church. "Whoever would be great among you must be your servant, and whoever would be first among you must be your slave" (Matt. 20:26–27). No one can deny that church history witnesses a great reversal of this apostolic order, so that ministries of service be-

came instruments of domination. Getting rid of every last vestige of
this authoritarian captivity of the ecclesiastical office is a necessary
condition of promoting the ecumenical hope of a mutual recognition
of ministries.

When the authoritarian model in doctrine and practice has been overcome by the relativizing impulse of our eschatological gospel, we will
have no trouble with the episcopal and papal ministries within the
church. These are offices that may witness to the marks of the church
and may serve to make them visible at every level of the church's life in
history. If they did not already exist, we would have to invent them for
theologically legitimate material reasons. We need to witness and minister to the unity of believers with the apostolic tradition, the unity of
believers with each other in the eucharistic fellowship of Christ, and the
unity of each congregation of believers with all other assemblies of God
in the world. This kind of ministry goes back to the apostles and has
always been needed in the church. These offices exist for the sake of what
is essential to the church; therefore in the sense of the historical and
eschatological categories we have used, the ordained ministries may so
be said to be servants of the *esse* and not only the *bene esse* of the church.

The Lutheran concentration on the gospel of Word and Sacraments as
the basis of the true unity of the church is compatible with the papal office but not with the papal claim—the infallibility claim. The Lutheran-
Catholic dialogues tackled this issue with lots of goodwill and erudition,
but finally reached the point of impasse.[10] We do not believe that the
highest office in the church possesses the infallibility of the Spirit at work
through the means of grace. Such a claim inherently leads to the abuse of
power in both church and world. The papal office, however, can serve
very well as a symbol and servant of the universal unity of the communities of faith working for the transformation of the world. The
various denominations could very well continue as distinct communities
in a new order so that just as there are Dominicans, Benedictines, and
Jesuits within the Roman Catholic Church, there will be Methodists,
Presbyterians, Lutherans, and others who may bring their best traditions
into a richer mix of the one holy, catholic, and apostolic church. The
negative aspects of denominationalism may be swallowed up and transcended by its positive aspects within a comprehensive unity of faith administered by a papal presidency and an episcopal magisterium.[11]

In the present ecumenical situation the next move is up to the pope, in-
asmuch as the unity of the church which his office exists to serve and to
symbolize is being obstructed by the dogmatic claims which have envel-

oped that office. By pressing the ecumenical dialogues back to the deep levels of apostolic faith, it may be possible for the gospel itself to remove the need once felt to buttress the papal office with the infallibility claim. We have received the gospel of the reign of God in fragile earthen vessels —our Scriptures, our creeds, our liturgies, and therefore also our ecclesiastical offices. All of these earthen vessels convey the sufficiency of God's grace and the unfailing power of his promises. These promises point forward to an eschatological future which radicalizes the relativity of the church in history. The power of this church of Christ is the power of the cross, not that of inerrant writings, infallible authorities, immutable dogmas, or absolute principles. It is the power of the cross that levels the ground on which all people and all structures stand in the church, so that all may become servants one of another, none lording it over the rest.

The hope of ecumenical progress toward reconciliation lies in a methodology that generates a vision of unity out of our common link to the apostolic gospel, and not first on a level of doctrinal statements, church administration, or ethical praxis. These latter things are not the stuff out of which the unity of the church is made, but rather give expression to that unity and keep the various members of the body moving in the unison of divine worship and world mission.

NOTES

1. "To the Christian Nobility of the German Nation, (1520)," *LW* 44:129.
2. Ibid.
3. This remark appears in Luther's fourteenth proposal for reform in his "To the Christian Nobility of the German Nation, (1520)," *LW* 44:175.
4. The most significant challenge to this view coming from within the Roman Catholic church has been written by Edward Schillebeeckx, *Ministry: Leadership in the Community of Jesus Christ* (New York: Crossroad, 1981).
5. Eric W. Gritsch and Robert W. Jenson, *Lutheranism: The Theological Movement and Its Confessional Writings* (Philadelphia: Fortress Press, 1976).
6. "To the Christian Nobility," *LW* 44:127–30.
7. The title of this address was "The Tragedy of the Reformation and the Return to Catholicity," printed in *The Record* of the Lutheran School of Theology (August 1965). An abridged version of this presentation was published under the title "Rome, Reformation, and Reunion," *Una Sancta* (June 1966), provoking a lot of both negative and positive response.
8. The ideas I was advancing at that time were very much influenced by the writings of George Lindbeck, whose thinking was far in advance of the rest of

Lutheranism. I was particularly stimulated by his article, "The Ecclesiology of the Roman Catholic Church," *Journal of Ecumenical Studies* 1, 2 (1964). The "exile" metaphor was suggested by this article.

9. Ernst Käsemann, "The Canon of the New Testament and the Unity of the Church," in *Essays on New Testament Themes* (Philadelphia: Fortress Press, 1982).

10. See the following books that came out of the dialogues on the papal office and its authority: Paul C. Empie and T. Austin Murphy, eds., *Papal Primacy and the Universal Church* (Minneapolis: Augsburg Publishing House, 1974). This was Dialogue V between Lutherans and Catholics. Dialogue VI was Paul C. Empie, T. Austin Murphy, and Joseph A. Burgess, eds., *Teaching Authority and Infallibility in the Church* (Minneapolis: Augsburg Publishing House, 1978). An earlier background study was issued: Raymond E. Brown, Karl P. Donfried, and John Reumann, eds., *Peter in the New Testament* (Minneapolis: Augsburg Publishing House, 1973).

11. See my chapter, "The Episcopate and the Petrine Office as Expressions of Unity," in Wolfhart Pannenberg, Avery Dulles, and Carl E. Braaten, *Spirit, Faith, and Church* (Philadelphia: Westminster Press, 1970), pp. 89–107.

4   *The Christocentric Principle*

THE LOGIC OF SALVATION

The chief aim of the church is to proclaim the gospel of God's salvation in Jesus Christ. Salvation is the most inclusive term for what the Bible declares God to have accomplished for the world through the person of Jesus. Every member of the church is called through baptism to witness to Jesus the Savior of humanity; every minister of the gospel is appointed through ordination to announce the good news of salvation within and outside the church. All Christians should agree to this. But there is no consensus in the church today on what salvation means and how it is to be procured. It is rather surprising that in two thousand years the church has never produced a dogma of salvation comparable to the dogmas of the Trinity or Christology. The nearest thing to it is the Lutheran doctrine of justification by grace alone, received through faith alone—the chief article of the Lutheran confessional writings.

One reason why there is no *specific* doctrine of salvation is that the whole of theology is inherently developed from a soteriological point of view. Salvation is not one of the many topics, along with the doctrine of God, Christ, church, sacraments, eschatology, and the like. It is rather the perspective from which all these subjects are interpreted, for the sake of the church's mission in the world. Another reason is that the meaning of salvation is subject to the relativity of historical experience so that theologians have expressed the one salvation in a multiplicity of symbols, related to particular times and places and various human needs and concerns.

Theology becomes boring and the church's preaching irrelevant when their interpretation of salvation loses touch with reality. When theology and the church address the deepest human questions, they are dealing with the theme of salvation even though the word is never mentioned. Yet specific language about salvation sounds strange in the modern world. Even within the church it is not altogether clear what preachers mean by their salvation talk, and if one happens to be attacked by the question of a street evangelist, "Are you saved?", the ordinary Christian is likely to feel uncomfortably at a loss for words. The whole subject of salvation is so awkward that many churches and preachers avoid the subject or find some appealing substitutes. An older person was overheard to have said, "Salvation is not what it used to be."

The churches and their preachers may be silent about salvation because they cannot see what difference it makes. Has Christian preaching of salvation noticeably changed the world? Do Christians look more saved than others? Can the history of Christianity be read as the achievement of salvation for the nations of the world? Has not salvation become an empty word? Is not this why some church groups desperately reach for every modern secular substitute for salvation, whether psychological for the individual person or more political for larger collectivities? Many of the fads of modern theology can be seen as frantic searches for a handle on salvation, intent on translating the gospel in modern terms. This is true of the very trendy movements in theology identified by words such as demythologizing, existentialism, secularization, death-of-God, psychedelic, process, revolution, feminist, liberation, and the parade of novelties that will surely continue. All of these have tried to translate Christian salvation in terms relevant to modern human experience; some have already died the death of such over-relevance that they end by feeding back into the situation nothing but what it has already discovered on its own.

The more deeply we probe the Christian sources for an answer to the soteriological questions posed by rugged experience and careful reflection in the fields of philosophy, psychology, and sociology, the more we find our focus of attention narrowing down to the traditional dogmatic topic of soteriology centering on the "work of Christ," and even more specifically on the doctrine of the atonement and the meaning of the death and resurrection of Jesus Christ. Soteriology—the doctrine of salvation—becomes inseparably linked to "Soter-ology"—the doctrine of the Savior. Here lies the truth in Philip Melanchthon's famous utterance: "To know Christ is to know his benefits."

Methodologically we cannot accept either the thinned out modern translations of the gospel of salvation, whether psychological or political, or the opaque repristinations of the ancient theories about salvation. Both are in dire need of the most careful hermeneutical treatment. Starting with the contemporary shape of the question concerning human salvation, we will quickly find ourselves in full-scale retreat from all the superficial modern answers back into the treasury of the tradition, to be challenged by both the depth of its witness to Christ and the scope of its symbols of interpretation in order to equip the church to proclaim a message that is absolutely unique, universal, decisive, and definitive of salvation for all humanity and the world.

The Christian doctrine of salvation moves between two hermeneutical poles. The first pole is the universal human need for salvation, anchored in the split nature of human existence, and expressed in various symbols and rites of all the religions. The second pole is the appearance of the Savior in history, who mediates the actual salvation human beings need. The knowledge of this salvation is transmitted through the Scriptures and the traditions of the church. If both poles are dialectically related, two opposite sorts of error can be avoided. The first is the subjectivist error of constructing the picture of the Christ solely from the side of human interests and desires for salvation. Then Christology becomes the mere objectification of soteriological ideas generated out of religious experience; these ideas are then projected onto the figure of a Jesus whose history is largely a matter of indifference. The second is the objectivist error which negates the formative part that the experience of saving faith and apostolic preaching played in the construction of the gospel picture of the Messiah Jesus. Then Christology becomes a system of facts and doctrines true in themselves, without reference to the structure of human experience.

The need for salvation is universal. Every religion presupposes that human beings need the salvation enshrined in their sacred mysteries. Christianity is no exception. But there are many ways to symbolize the lack in the human condition which salvation is supposed to meet. The fact of symbolic pluralism, however, need not negate the usefulness of an attempt to define the problematic elements of our common human existence. Underlying the plurality of dreams, yearnings, desires, hopes, and aspirations for salvation, typical of human beings wherever and whenever they happen to exist, there is a basic split in the structure of human existence. The self is divided; one side exists here and now with all its needs and lacks, the other side will and should exist in a state of fullness and satisfaction.

The idea of salvation, not only specifically Christian salvation, presupposes some kind of dualism in the human condition. If there were no split, if people were already whole, there would be no need for salvation, and religions and churches would simply go out of business, as they surely are destined to do in the biblical vision of the eternal kingdom of God.

There are several related facets of the universal split in the human condition. The first is the religious intuition that the end of earthly existence is not really the final end. Deep within the earthbound soul there is a yearning for a supernatural life beyond that will never end. There are various symbols of this other realm: immortality, reincarnation, resurrection, and the like. All of these picture a future state of bliss beyond this transitory existence.

A second facet of the divided self is the moral sense that life as we experience it should not end like this. It ought to be qualitatively different. This awareness of a transcendent imperative built into existence can express itself as protest against the miseries of this present age. This moral sense is also the source of the prophetic critiques of evil and the history of rebellion against slavery.

A third facet takes the form of concrete action to change the conditions of this imperfect world through educational enlightenment and social reform. The creative imagination can actively create a social world of life and meaning on top of the natural world of physical existence which humans share with the animals. But human beings long for a perfect community which has never been actualized, yet which has a higher right to exist than the unequal, unjust, unpeaceful, and unfulfilling forms of social history. Salvation has a communal dimension; the self is never without other selves.

The place to start our thinking about human salvation is in the midst of this two-dimensional life in which human beings cope with the everyday demands of their earthly existence and simultaneously transcend this world through ideas, symbols, images, rites, sacraments, and the like, of quite another world. As human beings we understand ourselves as citizens of two worlds. The modern one-dimensional dogma that we are only physical beings with nothing but our natural existence living in a self-contained secular world is one of the most unbelievable myths ever. There are, in fact, very few people who believe that, and they are mostly the victims of scientific reductionism. There is no such thing as a secular world void of the sacral dimensions in life which express the human quest for salvation. There is no world from which God is absent and in which he does not stir up a longing for the salvation which he alone can bring.

The world of the religions is filled with images of salvation that intersect with the everyday struggles of ordinary people. There is the image of returning to a lost state of nature, of paradise regained, of getting back to Eden. There is the image of going forward to the Promised Land, of coming home to the New Jerusalem, or entering a utopian heaven here on earth. There is the image of rising above this world, being transported into a kingdom of heaven somewhere. The list of the places of salvation is nearly endless, considering the stories about Olympus, Empyrium, Atlantis, Elysium, Valhalla, Nirvana, and the like. Likewise, a brief survey of the religions shows that the times of salvation are indefinite. When is this salvation real? It may be soon; it may be way in the past; or it may be sometime in the remote future. At times the feeling of aching nostalgia is dominant, at others a feverish expectation of coming salvation takes over. All the symbols of salvation are painted in marked contrast to earthly life as we know it. Salvation is elsewhere and at another time, or if it is here and now, it is hidden in another dimension beyond ordinary experience and therefore available only through faith or mystical experience. Faith is oriented to "things unseen," and mysticism comes from *muein*, meaning "eyes closed." We can see the logic of salvation at work in all these symbols and stories about salvation: the negation of the negative and the positing of the positive.

THE CONTEMPORARY SHAPE OF
THE SOTERIOLOGICAL QUESTION

Many of the traditional religious symbols and stories of salvation have become strange or dead to modern people. This is also true of the Judeo-Christian history of salvation in which Western civilization is rooted. A shift in the symbolism of salvation has taken place. Religious images of salvation that picture a radically different world in another time and place in which happiness, harmony, peace, and justice ultimately reign seem to have lost their power to convey reality. A chasm seems to have opened up between traditional salvation and modern reality. The dualistic structure of the mind which pictures another realm of power and meaning to ground and direct human life in this world seems to have been severely crippled so that we face a choice between two grim prospects. The first still optimistically holds out the hope of salvation, but within the limits of this world alone. Human beings can and will work out their own salvation. Salvation is a human project, subject to human planning and praxis. If these optimists are part of the establishment, they prefer an evolutionary road to salvation; it takes a long time and little has to change meanwhile. If they are part of the proletariat, they may prefer a revolutionary model; they have good reason to speed up the coming of the time when they can get their share of the salvation this world has to offer.

The second prospect is the pessimistic loss of hope for this world. There are no divine or human ideals with power to influence this world for the better. The keynote sounded by many philosophers and authors has been the "meaninglessness of human existence." Born into a meaningless world, we will all come to a meaningless end. All efforts to announce the hope of salvation are superstition.

The major shift in the symbolism of salvation took place in the age of the Enlightenment as a shift from a theocentric to an anthropocentric focus. It is a downward shift from the "City of God" to the "City of Man," from an eschatological view of salvation in which God is the sole source of salvation to a this-worldly, humanistic focus on human happiness and social welfare. Religion may still fit into this new worldview as long as it integrates itself into a reasonable definition of the good life on earth. Religious language tends to become indistinguishable from the artificial discourses on enlightened utopianism. Even within the tough exterior of revolutionary Marxism there is a soft utopian vision of a future for the masses where there will be no more cries of unemployment, poverty, hunger, want, and care, no more wage slavery and exploitation by the ruling capitalistic class. The eschatological reign of God in a new heaven and a new earth has become a utopian belief in "peace on earth, good will toward men."

In the post-Enlightenment situation the main elements emerging in the overall picture of modern salvation have been reason and nature, contributed chiefly by a blend of rationalism and romanticism in the eighteenth century; then justice and peace, energetically proposed by socialism and Marxism in the nineteenth century; and finally progress and development, which have harnessed science and technology in the hopes of building one universal culture for the good of all peoples and nations. It has become difficult for modern people to speak of salvation in any other terms.

The soteriological shift is an earthward shift from superhuman to human power, from an eschatological image of salvation above and beyond history to a utopian picture of possibilities inherent in this world, from a transcendental providence directing history to an immanent process of world-historical development. The interesting differences in this respect between Voltaire and Rousseau, or between Kant and Lessing, or between Comte and Darwin, or between Marx and Mao, all appear minuscule from a soteriological point of view compared to the difference between a belief in salvation based on human power and one that trusts in the power of God. The image of salvation is bound to be weakened by a loss of faith in providence and eschatology; it leaves human beings to make their own history of salvation without the help of God. At first, this shift appears to endow human beings with new dignity, putting into their hands what traditionally belonged solely to the power of God. The twentieth century will be remembered as the period when human beings began to realize that they do not handle the job of being God to themselves very well. When salvation fell into their hands, they began also no longer to believe in themselves. They became afflicted by doubt and despair, found themselves without meaning or goal, lost conscience and courage, and contracted a sickness unto death, a belief in the valuelessness of human beings. How else will posterity account for the fact that in the twentieth century, civilization prepared to extinguish itself by using the tools of that very enlightenment by which it declared itself liberated from belief in God? Human beings are learning that a world in which God is declared dead is becoming a dangerous place in which to live.

THE SPECTRUM OF SALVATION

Some churches and theologies have tried to define Christian salvation within the framework of the post-Enlightenment worldview. They have tried to pour the old wine of salvation into the new skins of secularism. The most absurd instance of this approach was the death-of-God theology which died about a decade ago now. Process theology and liberation theology, the two leading schools of theology in America today, appear less absurd only because they succeed better in disguising their commitment to an image of salvation confined totally within the limits of this world and our modern, enlightened understanding of reason and nature, justice and peace, progress and development—all predicates of possibilities immanent in the world as it is here and now.

In current theology there is a renaissance of the Old Testament perspective in soteriology. To many it seems more directly relevant to the modern situation. There is no "pie in the sky by and by" in the religion of Israel. On this side of the caesura of secularization it seems more natural to find a biblical point of contact for "modern man" within the Old Testament. It is no secret that liberation theology takes most of its images of salvation from the experience of Israel in history, revolving around Exodus and exile. Not much is said about the human situation in light of Eden and *eschaton*—the absolute beginning and end of human being in the world.

Israel was essentially agnostic when it came to questions concerning life after death. The chief concern was for a this-worldly future and not another world. Immortality was conceived of in terms of perpetuating the name and the race; the people of Israel would become more numerous than the sands of the sea or the stars of the sky. The charter of Israel's existence was the covenant, but the promises of the covenant referred to Israel's future on this earth. We look in vain for clear references to resurrection and eternal life. Neither is there any stress on individual salvation, only on the perpetuation of the people. Death is not the great divide, nor is heaven the ultimate end in Israel's thinking about God and human destiny. The ultimate goal is glory on earth, if not for this generation, at least for the generations to come. All of this seems so readily reducible to the this-worldly limits of salvation imposed on religion in a secular age.

The Old Testament provides a point of contact also for the soteriological shift to a social-ethical definition of religion. The prophet of Israel is a champion of the poor, the oppressed, and the weak. He is the advocate of social reform, the leader of the righteous opposition, attacking kings and priests, rich men and loose women. The prophet is a man of the common people, interested solely in lifting up the masses.

What, then, is salvation? It is a tangible paradise on earth; it is a land flowing with milk and honey; it is all living creatures, every tree and flower, every rock, river and mountain—all nature—glowing with the goodness and glory of a perfected world. The human heart will become new, receiving a new spirit. Israel—the despised, rejected, and persecuted nation—will be exalted above all the mightiest powers of the world. Salvation is deliverance, liberation, perfection, starting with Israel and reaching to the ends of the earth. This will not simply fall into the lap of Israel, for Israel is called upon to do her part. There will be no salvation without a new life of repentance, responsibility, and righteousness. The synergism built into this model of salvation may partly account for its attractiveness to liberation and process theologians, who base salvation on a synthesis of divine and human actions.

Theology must go back before it can go forward, back behind the Enlightenment and beyond the captivity of salvation within the limits of the post-Enlightenment world view. The question of salvation will arise in every human situation, also within the limits of our modern world view, but the answer which comes from the Christian tradition must be allowed to deepen the question and shatter every world view if we hope to understand the meaning and scope of the Christian doctrine of salvation.

The liberation model of salvation that is so popular in both psychologically and politically oriented schools of thought is totally silent about the deep themes we find in classical theories of the atonement. I have in mind such themes as "bought with a price," "a ransom for many," "re-capitulation," "God was in Christ, reconciling the world to himself," "expiation for the sins of the whole world," "sacrifice," and the like. These are a few of the biblical concepts that stirred the imagination of the greatest theologians in the Christian tradition: Irenaeus, Origen, Gregory of Nyssa, Athanasius, Augustine, Anselm, Thomas, Luther, Calvin. They are the mountain peaks. Theology today is in a valley of dry bones when it comes to answering Anselm's question, *Cur deus homo*? Or Irenaeus's *Ut quid enim descendebat*? What does it mean to say that Jesus died *for us*? What is the significance of the atoning death of Jesus and his resurrection?

Scholars have attempted to deal with the history of the Christian doctrine of salvation in typological terms. The various types correspond to periods in the history of theology. Hence, F. C. Baur distinguished three periods related in a dialectical scheme, reflecting his Hegelian perspective: the mystical (the Greek fathers of the East), the juridical (the Latin fathers of the West), and the moral (modern Protestant theology).[1] The most famous typology is perhaps that of Gustaf Aulén, who also discovered a triad of motifs: the *Christus victor* motif of the ancient fathers, the *Christus victima* motif of medieval theology, and the *Christus exemplar* motif of modern Protestantism.[2]

There is much to be said for the typological approach. But there are some pitfalls which need to be kept in mind. The typological approach leaves the impression that a choice must be made among them. The church has never seen fit to make a doctrinal decision on the atonement. The spectrum of salvation in the church's preaching from the Scriptures, in its liturgical traditions, and in its devotional materials is far too pluralistic to be pressed into the mold of a single theory. Nor can the thought of any classical theologian be reduced to one common denominator.

The theology of salvation must be as multidimensional as the supreme act of God in Christ surely is, involving the entire spectrum of saving events in the gospel story of Jesus—his birth, his life and teachings, his death and resurrection, his ascension and session at the right hand of God, and his final coming in glory to judge the living and the dead. Soteriology must be multidimensional also because it corresponds to the many dimensions of human existence in the world, individual and corporate, and all sorts of needs and conditions. No one theory of redemption can cover the whole story of the relationship between God and the world in the person of the mediator Jesus Christ.

Another factor is that each epoch favors one particular set of metaphors that makes sense within the horizon of its own peculiar life situation. In the patristic age Jesus is pictured as the Logos who culminates a long pedagogical process in history, bringing a new doctrine, a new example, even the true philosophy. Knowledge (*gnosis*) was the human need, and so Jesus was the *Christos didaskalos*—the divine pedagogue.[3] In the medieval period salvation was more readily expressed in analogy with the feudal order, as an act of restoring the divinely ordained order of things that had been broken by sin. Anselm of Canterbury built up his idea of salvation on this basis. Similarly, the various modern models or theories, as different as they may be, reflect the modern drive to freedom deeply rooted in modern subjectivity. Thus, Jesus becomes the liberator or "Jesus means freedom,"[4] and as such the medium of the self-fulfillment of the human subject.

Without negating the elements of meaning in the various classical theories of atonement, I have formulated my own preference in what I wrote as a "little dogmatic," *The Future of God*,[5] under the heading "Jesus: God's Representative and Ours." The reader may notice a striking resemblance to the title of one of Dorothee Soelle's books, *Christ the Representative*,[6] which develops a notion that had previously been proposed by Wolfhart Pannenberg in his *Jesus: God and Man*[7] in a section entitled "Jesus as Representative of Men Before God." However, I do not limit myself to the structure of their ideas. Soelle tries to move within the limits of Christian atheism and thus has no doctrine of God, and Pannenberg stresses Jesus' functional solidarity with all human beings in his relation to God. I have taken both sides of Jesus' role as representative, God's and ours. Only then can this notion be fully useful for the doctrine of salvation.

I intend not to repeat what I have written elsewhere on the subject of representation, but only to summarize a few salient ideas. The most important notion, common to preaching, piety, and dogmatics, is that "Christ died for us." This is the *sine qua non* of every doctrine of atonement. In dying for us, Jesus did not die instead of us, for we all still have to die. In suffering for us, he did not suffer instead of us, for we all have to suffer. Yet he represents us before God. He speaks for us when we are silenced by death. He claims that each of us is unique, indispensable, and absolutely irreplaceable even though the world treats us as expendable and exchangeable and as mere statistical units. Here we have the solid ground of personal identity free of charge, while people are madly searching for security in a supermarket full of answers with high price tags. In this world in which the value of individual human beings is becoming infinitesimally low, Jesus is our representative in his life and in his vicarious death and in his victorious resurrection.

Faith is an act of letting Jesus be our representative. Because he died for us, we never die alone without representation, without hope for personal identity beyond the grave. We will never have to die alone on a Godforsaken hill outside the gate. We can die in a communion of his love, in the assurance of the forgiveness of sins, with undying hope for resurrection and eternal life. Because Jesus died the death of the sinner as the sinless one, assuming our lot by his love, he can be our representative. Because he died the death under the law as the man of love, full of life to share and taking time for others, he can be our representative. He can be our representative because, in being raised from the dead, he was approved by God as having the right credentials to be the ambassador of the human race.

That is the one side. The other is that Jesus is also God's representative. Jesus represents the full value of God's love for us in a world short of the right kind of love. In Jesus' suffering, God himself is taking part in the pain of each one of us. Jürgen Moltmann's *The Crucified God*[8] is the profoundest book on this topic in contemporary theology. The idea that God cannot participate in human suffering and death is a heresy worse than patripassianism, because it contradicts the gospel itself. Bonhoeffer's words struck the right note: "Only a suffering God can help."[9]

It used to be thought that only human beings were in trouble and needed to have someone to plead their case before God. This is what kept priests in business. In light of the gospel, God also needs to have a representative to plead his case before humanity. The Old Testament is full of arguments in which God seeks to justify himself before those who would accuse him of being a do-nothing God. God is also on trial. He longs for his people to honor him only with love and service to his creation. Jesus is the only answer to the problem of theodicy; he is God's chosen representative to make his case credible in a world of pain and death.

PERMANENT ELEMENTS IN
A THEOLOGY OF SALVATION

The history of the doctrine of salvation and the various typological constructions make us aware of the variable elements. They should not blind us to the constant elements which give us a standard or norm by which to measure the adequacy of any soteriological proposal. Here I would wish to propose a checklist—a kind of ten commandments—of what must constitute a Christian doctrine of salvation.

1. *Only God can save.* Human beings cannot save themselves, no matter how hard they try. Every synergistic doctrine of salvation is a heresy even though the majority of Christian denominations are guilty of overt or covert synergism.

2. *God's only saving bridge to the world is Jesus the Christ.* He alone is the saving mediator between God and the world. The gospel says there is no other name on earth by which people can be saved.

3. *An understanding of the atonement must take seriously the polarity between the justice and the love of God.* Love without justice is sentimentality, and justice without love makes salvation of a guilty world impossible.

4. *The whole life of Christ from incarnation through resurrection must be taken into account.* The mathematical point of the cross cannot bear the whole brunt of salvation even though the atonement centers in the cross of Jesus.

5. *The atonement is a once-for-all act which is inherently and antecedently valid, prior to any subjective response on the part of believers.* Faith does not produce the meaning of the salvation event; it can only receive it in radical gratitude.

6. *The human condition consists in sin as a guiltiness before the living God which can be rectified only by divine forgiveness.* Christocentric salvation has revealed that the human condition in its radical extremity consists of more than human finitude, social injustice, or existential anxiety.

7. *God's way of salvation is by identification with sinful humanity.* In classical atonement doctrine, he became what we are in order that we might become what he is. Luther similarly spoke of the "happy exchange" in which God in Christ exchanges place with sinners so that sinners might share gratis the righteousness of God (cf. 2 Cor. 5:21).

8. *In Christ God saves the whole human race, not one individual at a time.* The whole of humankind is a family; we are all in Adam's boat through original and hereditary sin (cf. 1 Cor. 15:22).

9. *God in Christ bears the whole guilt of sin and all its consequences.*

The sinless Christ suffered the punishment of our sin; his is therefore a vicarious suffering (cf. John 1:29).

10. *The cross of Christ is a victory over the tyrants which oppress the world.* Salvation must mean liberation from the power of the evil one and all his works and ways. The cross is a victory over the power of the demonic. By suffering at the hands of evil, he conquers it.

JUSTIFICATION AND LIBERATION

Liberation theology is currently proposing a new paradigm of salvation. It is timely and appealing, but I wonder if it is sufficiently cogent and convincing. Liberation theology is right to focus on the wretchedness of the human condition, although it has in mind chiefly the misery of the poor and the oppressed. Liberation theology is right to work for the overthrow of all systems of domination which exploit and enslave people, although it tends to look through the narrow peephole of the class conflict in society. Liberation theology is right to call for the transformation of society and not to tolerate the situation of injustice, poverty, and oppression generated by the social system, although its rhetoric of denunciation, as with the prophets of Israel, is more clear than its alternative vision of the new. But what do the liberation movements of whatever ilk, that promise to change the world for the better, have to do with the salvation which Christianity announces in the name of God's gospel about Jesus' cross and resurrection?

The kind of salvation that liberation theology lifts up is generally something Athens could in principle discover without the help of Jerusalem, something Marx in fact called for without reference to Jesus, something which will come about through human praxis without any necessary dependence on God's act in Christ. This is its advantage, because it does not require Christians for its success. In light of Marx's idea of praxis, which liberation theologians use as a tool of analysis, the notion of God's saving act in Christ is, strictly speaking, bound to be viewed as a fetish. Praxis means a new course of action to change the world. Salvation awaits the outcome. Meanwhile there is only the class conflict. The call to conversion is now the call to join the struggle on the left side. The Christian is free to do this, of course. It is then a practical ethical decision which falls under Luther's rubric, *"pecca fortiter."* It most certainly does not constitute what Christian faith means by *soteria*.

Liberation theology has made an option for socialistic salvation which shares the classical liberal vision of a society built on the principles of freedom and justice, and finally a society in which no group or class is dominated and oppressed by others. Actually, the original roots of these liberal social ideals stem from the Stoic concept of human nature but are also intertwined with the Christian-biblical vision of the kingdom of God bringing in a reign of peace and righteousness. It is not these noble ideals which disqualify the socialist model of salvation from a Christian soteriological perspective but its underlying optimistic view of the human condition. Such a view contradicts the biblical estimate that sin and evil lie deep in the infrastructure of every person. Moreover, the socialist plan of salvation, which trusts that by getting rid of the private ownership of the means of production we will gain the cash value of God's kingdom in earthly terms, also stands in contradiction to the biblical view. The Christian hope of salvation is deeply suspicious of all political promises—from the left or the right or the middle—to inaugurate a world of freedom, peace, and justice. Only God will bring in such a world. A down payment on this new world has already been made in the Christ event and is proleptically embodied in the audible sacraments and visible words by means of which the church bears witness to eschatological salvation.

The liberationist idea of praxis is very seductive. Since Christian salvation *sola gratia* has failed to change the world, why not try a new approach—not faith, but praxis? Why leave it to God and do nothing? Why not adopt Marxist praxis as a lever to get things going in the right way? Christianity has used philosophical concepts in other situations, like the Stoic *logos*, the Aristotelian *summum bonum*,. the Hegelian *Geist*, the Heideggerian *Existenz*, the Whiteheadian *process*, so why not Marxist *praxis?* True enough, but they have all proved nearly disastrous for Christian theology. It has often happened in history that the threat to Christian identity does not arise from those who explicitly attack it from the outside but from those who launch an invasion of Christianity in a Trojan horse. Only when the horse is inside the walls of Troy does the hatch open and do Agamemnon and all the rest jump out and capture the city. The Marxist critique of religion as opium has not been able to succeed. But if its theory of praxis can spread inside the body of Christianity, it might be able to claim victory at last. With all the lessons of the past, theologians today ought to recognize that praxis is no magic key to open the way of salvation. This does not mean that the idea of praxis is useless, only that it must be baptized, that is, transformed under the impact of the gospel of salvation.

I believe the soteriological deficit in the liberationist paradigm of salvation coincides with the turn away from Paul in contemporary theology and back to the historical Jesus. Paul stands for a soteriology that is oriented to the cross and resurrection of Jesus, whereas Jesus stands for the kingdom of God, which has only to be de-eschatologized, and particularly de-apocalypticized, to make it fit a this-worldly, inner-historical, socio-ethical interpretation of the kingdom. Many people feel that Paul's problem is no longer ours and that therefore his answers are bound to seem foreign to us. They feel that modern people do not suffer from the pressure of religious guilt but rather from the pressure of work, the competitive society, and the political system. They seek freedom and liberation as much as ever, but they do not expect to find it by faith alone, as Paul proposed. Instead, they expect to find it by really changing the social structures.

Is it possible to unwrap the bandages that hide Paul's message in the thought categories of the first century and release it for an encounter with the needs of people seeking salvation today? Paul's message centered in justification through faith apart from the works of the law. Some scholars have disputed the centrality of justification in Paul's thought. Wrede called it a polemical doctrine against the Judaizers, and Schweitzer merely a "side crater." Käsemann, however, has renewed our confidence that justification through faith was at the heart of Paul's gospel.[10] This was the view of the Reformers, and I believe they were basically right. The Reformation spoke of the article of justification as the *articulus stantis et cadentis ecclesiae*. It is more than that, for if it lies at the gospel's center, it has to do fundamentally with the standing and falling of not only the church but of the whole of humanity. The Christian doctrine of salvation takes its stand on the doctrine of justification in conflict with all other systems of salvation presented by the ideologies and religions of the world, and is not limited in relevance to the controversy between the Reformation and Roman Catholicism.

The core of justification is the freedom which Paul announces in letter after letter. This freedom is multidimensional; it has personal, ecclesial, and cosmic elements of meaning. It means freedom from the law, from sin, and finally from death. Paul summed it up: "For freedom Christ has set us free" (Gal. 5:1). This freedom in Christ has both an eschatological and an ethical aspect. This freedom is a gift of God; it cannot be gained by sweating it out under the law. Justification and freedom are two sides of the same act of God in Christ. This is the article of faith which can deepen and correct the liberation model of salvation, for all the liberating praxis in history can do nothing to produce love and freedom and can do nothing about human bondage to sin and death. The Pauline-Reformation doctrine of justification reveals the truth of the human situation before God—humanity in the grip of sin, death, and the power of the demonic. It also places the full burden of salvation from this bondage squarely on the shoulders of the crucified and risen Savior. Liberation in social, political, and economic terms, legitimate and desirable as this is to strive for, cannot be the whole of salvation since it cannot touch the tyrants which have met their match only in the encounter with Jesus Christ our Lord.

THE UNIVERSAL MEANING OF JESUS CHRIST

The Christian believes that Jesus Christ is the one and only Savior of the world. Acts 4:12 says it so clearly: "And there is salvation in no one else, for there is no other name under heaven given among men by which we must be saved." As a child I used to wonder what my parents were doing on the Godforsaken island of Madagascar out in the Indian Ocean. The missionaries, my parents and teachers, cited this Bible verse (Acts 4:12) as explanation. And they linked it with another, Rom. 10:14: "But how are men to call upon him in whom they have not believed? And how are they to believe in him of whom they have never heard? And how are they to hear without a preacher?" The missionaries were there to preach the gospel so that the heathen might believe and be saved. That seemed to make a lot of sense.

Like many others growing up with this evangelical belief, I was not far advanced in Sunday school before I began to worry about all who did not believe and belong to the church, the millions who live and die with no chance to hear the gospel. Are they all lost? Will they go to hell? Will only those be saved in the end who hear the gospel, believe in Christ, and belong to his church? Will only Christians be saved at last?

One of the most hotly debated topics in modern theology is whether there is salvation apart from the Christian faith, whether other religions possess saving knowledge of God, indeed, whether even humanists and atheists can be saved if they live up to the best within their reach.

Since the beginning, Christianity has made an exclusive claim. The traditional Catholic type of exclusiveness has claimed: "There is no salvation outside the church" (*extra ecclesiam nulla salus*). Pope Boniface VIII in 1302 said: "We believe that there is one holy catholic and apostolic church outside of which there is no salvation." He even went so far as to say that by church he had in mind the *Roman* Catholic church. "We declare that it is necessary for salvation for every human creature to be subject to the Roman Pontiff."[11] Protestants have rejected that claim, but they have countered with their own evangelical version of exclusiveness. They have stated that apart from faith there is no salvation, faith only in the gospel, which comes from hearing, just as hearing comes from preaching. Roman Catholics and evangelical Protestants have a long tradition of exclusiveness. Whatever it is they typically stress, that and that *alone* is for them the way of salvation.

Hearing it stated so boldly, many have cringed at the consequences of their own exclusivistic assertions. Will only *bona fide* Roman Catholics be saved? No. There are loopholes. Roman Catholics have created the infamous loopholes of "invincible ignorance" and "baptism by desire." That means there is hope for a Protestant, or a Buddhist for that matter, if sufficiently ignorant. That means that I will be saved if I would have desired baptism, had I been in a situation to have been offered a chance. God, who is all-knowing, knows of course what would have happened if what did happen had not happened. So there is a big loophole for lots of people, after all, outside the Roman Catholic church. I call this hypothetical salvation—a pretty chancy business.

Protestants have not much liked the Roman Catholic loopholes. But they have invented some of their own. The old Lutheran dogmaticians could not quite get themselves to believe that Socrates, Plato, Aristotle, and other such noble pagans would roast in hell for eternity. Although Protestants clearly taught there is salvation through faith in Christ alone, they could not quite believe that people in Old Testament times or other people in far-flung parts of the world outside of earshot of the gospel would necessarily be damned forever. They found a loophole in the Bible, in 1 Pet. 3:19, which states that Christ preached to the spirits in prison. This is the basis of their belief that people who did not hear the gospel in this life would be given a second chance. There is something to commend this doctrine of the second chance. Even in baseball, which is only for fun or money, you get three chances to hit the ball. Now if eternal life is at stake, why not at least a second chance, especially if you are so unlucky as to have been born on the Sandwich Islands before Christianity began to send missionaries around the world.

Even the Billy Graham evangelicals, who normally sound extremely

exclusivistic, cannot tolerate the literal consequences of their own position. They claim that all are lost who do not make a conscious decision
for Christ. So they teach believer's baptism. Only those who first believe
and then are baptized will be saved. But what about infants? What about
the mentally retarded? They are not accountable. They have not reached
the age of rational accountability. So they have a chance to be assigned
to some limbo or other. When you scratch these evangelicals a little, you
find they are all rationalists beneath the skin, and not very biblical after
all. When pressed, they invent their own kind of loophole.

Is there any other way but for Christians to insist on exclusive salvation and invent a loophole or two, either of the Roman Catholic or of the
Protestant type? Some Christians and theologians have seen the sham in
claiming exclusiveness on the one hand and creating loopholes on the
other. Is there a way to be more consistent? Today some are proposing
that we drop the exclusive claim and along with it the need for loopholes.
Why not simply affirm full and equal salvation in all the religions? Why
not acknowledge that all the major religions do their share in offering
people the way of salvation?

A British professor, John Hick of Birmingham University, has renewed
the age-old controversy about whether there is salvation only through
Christ. In several writings, he clearly denies it.[12] He denies that Jesus
Christ *alone* is the way of salvation. That takes care of the Christian root
of exclusivism. John Hick and others like him deny that God can be
known adequately *only* through Jesus. He claims, instead, that Jesus is
only one of the many ways that lead to the one God of the universe. To
be sure, Jesus is still valid as the Christian's way, but other religions
possess equally valid ways. There are Catholics too who call for the end
of Christian exclusiveness. Paul Knitter, for example, challenges Christians to abandon the narrow claim that Jesus Christ is different, decisive,
unique, normative, and final. This narrow claim, he says, makes Christians closed-minded, unfit for the age of pluralism and the coming
dialogue between the world's major religions, so essential for peace in
the global village.

So we seem to be confronted by two equally unattractive options. The
exclusivistic option, whether of the Protestant or the Catholic type, gives
us small hope for the world in the end. The new universalistic option
puts Christ into a pantheon of world saviors. I am convinced these common options are based on a defective Christology; their thinking about
Christ is too small.

The New Testament is the only document which gives us a reliable picture of Jesus of Nazareth, who he is and what he means. He is clearly depicted as the Messiah of Israel, God's only Son, the Lord of creation, and the Savior of all humanity. The New Testament abounds with titles which identify the uniqueness of Jesus. It is simply not possible to say with Hick and Knitter that we can subtract these titles from the picture of the man and have any real Jesus at all. We have no picture of Jesus as merely Jesus, to interpret as we please. The only Jesus we know is Jesus *as* the Christ, Son of God, Logos, Lord, Savior—all titles of highest possible honor, putting him in the place which Israel had reserved for God alone, so much so that ultimately the church's trinitarian formula became the only sound way to speak about the identity and meaning of Jesus. This shuts the door against the christological relativism of the new universalism. If we read the New Testament aright, we learn that Jesus is not *a* son of God, but the *only* Son, not *a* savior, but the *only* Savior, not *a* lord, but *the* Lord of lords, and so on. Nothing is more certain in the New Testament than its intention to picture Jesus in an utterly exclusive way, making this claim the heart of the gospel itself. In answer to John the Baptist's question, "Are you the one who is to come?" the good-news answer is "Yes, and we need not look for another."

Jesus is uniquely unique. Of course, each one of us is unique. I am the only one of me who has ever existed. As an individual human being Jesus is unique in this general sense too. But he is also unique in a sense different from the rest of us. He is like us in every respect (sin excepting), but he is also very much unlike us; so he is properly designated the living Christ, the risen Lord, the final Judge, the eschatological Savior of the world. This way of speaking cannot apply to us, not even to the human race as a whole. Only Jesus is the legitimate subject of such titles of exaltation.

The special quality of Jesus' uniqueness is best grasped in terms of his universal meaning. This concrete person, Jesus of Nazareth, is unique because of his unequalled universal significance. The point of his uniqueness underlines his universality. If Jesus is *the* Lord and Savior, he is the *universal* Lord and Savior, not merely my *personal* Lord and Savior. Because Jesus is the unique and universal Savior, there is a large hope for salvation, not only for me and others with the proper credentials of believing and belonging to the church, but for all people whenever or wherever they might have lived and no matter how religious or irreligious they may have proved themselves to be.

It is clearly God's announced will that all people shall be saved and come to the knowledge of truth (1 Tim. 2:4). Evangelicals generally admit this, except the hard-nosed Calvinists among them who still teach a limited atonement, namely, that Christ died only for the elect, the lucky few predestined for salvation. But evangelicals also generally deny that God's will to save all will come to pass in the end. God's will to universal salvation will be frustrated in the end. So they say. But is it true? If Jesus Christ is the sole medium of our knowledge of God's will in matters of salvation, can we be so sure that the one who lived and died for all was not granted the promise of eschatological victory by his resurrection from the dead? If we dare to be universalists in our hope for the salvation of the totality of the world and of humankind, it is because our hope reflects the size, not merely of our faith, but of the Christ whose identity the New Testament loudly proclaims in universally significant terms.

The Christian hope for salvation, whether for the believing few or the unbelieving many, is grounded in the person and meaning of Christ alone—not in the potential of the world's religions to save or in the moral seriousness of humanists and people of goodwill or even in the good works of pious Christians and church people, who perhaps are compulsively believing too many things and going to church more than is good for them.

If our hope of universal salvation had no basis in the Bible, there would remain only a flimsy thread of well-meaning speculation on which to hang it. The church father, Origen of Alexandria, was the past master of the kind of universalism that springs from pure metaphysical speculation. But the final destiny of humanity is too serious a thing for theology to make a toy of speculation. If it is worth holding at all, it must be in terms of the faith, hope, and love generated by nothing less than the New Testament and its gospel about Jesus the Christ of God.

There is a universalist thrust in the New Testament, particularly in the Pauline theology. How else can we read passages such as the following: "For as in Adam all die, so also in Christ shall all be made alive" (1 Cor. 15:22). "For in him (Christ) all the fullness of God was pleased to dwell, and through him to reconcile to himself all things, whether on earth or in heaven, making peace by the blood of his cross" (Col. 1:19–20). "For he has made known to us in all wisdom and insight the mystery of his will, according to his purpose which he set forth in Christ as a plan for the fullness of time, to unite all things in him, things in heaven and things on earth" (Eph. 1:9–10). There are numerous other such statements that point to the universal scope of Christ's meaning. The most intriguing is in 1 Cor. 15:28: "When all things are subjected to him, then the Son himself will also be subjected to him who put all things under him, that God may be everything to every one." This is the biblical base for what in technical theology is called eschatological panentheism (not pantheism).

Why is it that there is salvation for humanity and the world only through Christ? Why cannot we equate Christian salvation with Buddhist illumination or with Hindu unification or with some variant of the human potential movement or with the Marxist transformation of the world through revolution or with anything else which one of the religions or ideologies chooses to call salvation? The reason is that salvation in the New Testament is not some vague feeling of fulfillment, not the filling of every kind of need, not a reward for heroic effort, not the realization of one's human potential. Salvation in the New Testament is what God has done to death in the resurrection of Jesus. Salvation is what God has in store for you and me and the whole world in spite of death, solely on account of the living, risen Christ. This is the kerygma the apostles of Jesus preached, and this is what the fathers of the ancient church framed into dogma. If modern-day Christians or theologians choose to follow some other guide or guru, they are free to do so; but then they are moonlighting on their own, and no one in or outside the church need take them seriously.

It is inevitable that Christianity will enter into dialogue with the major non-Christian religions and secular ideologies of our time. Some believers will be seduced by the salvation claims they make and the spiritual experiences they produce. This is already happening as the exotic religious winds are blowing in from the East. At Newark airport I met a blonde girl witnessing to Krishna consciousness. She told me she had been baptized in a Lutheran church and later had tried the Pentecostal movement, but she found salvation only in Krishna consciousness. I asked, "What does Krishna do for you that Christ can't do?" She said, "They are one and the same." I asked, "But can you also say that Jesus is Krishna?" And she replied, "No way! Jesus was a physical being with a human body. And the body stinks. It is full of sores and scabs, mucus and disease, and it's all bound to die."

The universal scope of salvation in Christ includes the destiny of our bodies together with the whole earth and the whole of creation. This cosmic hope is based on the promise of eternal life sealed by the resurrection of Jesus from the dead. Through raising Jesus from the dead, God put death to death, overcoming the deadliest enemy of life at loose in the world. This hope for the final salvation of humanity and the eternal universal restitution of all things in heaven and on earth and below the earth is not based on any loophole invented by theologians. It is hope drawn from the unlimited promise of the gospel and the magnitude of God's grace made known to the world through Christ.

Will, then, all people be saved in the end? We do not already know the answer. The final answer is stored up in the mystery of God's own future. All he has let us know in advance is that he will judge the world according to the measure of his grace and love made known in Jesus Christ, which is ultimately greater than the fierceness of his wrath or the hideousness of our sin.

What about the stuff in the Bible concerning the sheep and the goats, all the passages pointing not to universalism, but to a division of the world into the saved and the lost? What about the stern warnings in the Bible threatening eternal perdition? This is the dark side. But these dark sayings are uttered not so much to frighten sinners as to disturb the complacency of the righteous—all the people with apparently the right credentials. Listen to these words. They are meant for people like us. "This people honors me with their lips, but their heart is far from me" (Matt. 15:8). "Not every one who says to me, 'Lord, Lord,' shall enter the kingdom of heaven" (Matt. 7:21). The New Testament is full of warnings of the spiritual danger of using the right evangelical words and correct ecclesiastical doctrines as a religious screen against the living Word and will of God. These warnings are the penultimate Word of God. The ultimate verdict has fallen once for all in the Christ of history, from the eternal future of God's all-encompassing love.

NOTES

1. Ferdinand Christian Baur, *Die christliche Lehre von der Versöhnung in ihrer geschichtlichen Entwicklung* (Tübingen: C. F. Osiander, 1838), p. 12

2. Gustaf Aulén, *Christus Victor*, trans. A. G. Herbert (New York: Macmillan Co., 1951).

3. Leo Schefczyk, ed., *Erlösung und Emanzipation* (Freiburg: Verlag Herder, 1973), pp. 72–83.

4. Ernst Käsemann, *Jesus Means Freedom* (Philadelphia: Fortress Press, 1969).

5. Carl E. Braaten, *The Future of God* (New York: Harper & Row, 1969).

6. Dorothee Soelle, *Christ the Representative* (Philadelphia: Fortress Press, 1967).

7. Wolfhart Pannenberg, *Jesus—God and Man* (Philadelphia: Westminster Press, 1968).

8. Jürgen Moltmann, *The Crucified God* (New York: Harper & Row, 1974).

9. Dietrich Bonhoeffer, *Letters and Papers from Prison* (New York: Macmillan Co., 1953), p. 220.

10. Ernst Käsemann, *Commentary on Romans*, trans. Geoffrey W. Bromiley (Grand Rapids, Mich.: Wm. B. Eerdmans, 1980).

11. *Unam Sanctam*, Papal Bull of Boniface VIII, 1302.

12. Cf. "Jesus and the World Religions," in John Hick, ed., *The Myth of God Incarnate* (Philadelphia: Westminster Press, 1977). See also Hick's book, *God and the Universe of Faiths* (New York: Macmillan Co., 1973).

5   The Sacramental Principle

THE PROTESTANT CAPTIVITY OF THE SACRAMENTS

There are signs that sacramental theology is on the upswing within the Protestant churches.[1] After the Reformation, Huldreich Zwingli's symbolic view of the sacraments gained wide circulation in the Reformed churches. Ecumenically speaking this view is now bankrupt, and many theologians within Protestantism have shifted their allegiance from Zwingli to the more realistic doctrines of John Calvin and Martin Luther. Lutheranism itself has not been immune to the anti-sacramental tendency of Protestant worship life. I have been in Lutheran churches where the Lord's Supper is celebrated only four times a year and where the chief concern is that grape juice be used instead of wine.

Paul Tillich was hardly exaggerating when he wrote about the "death of the sacraments" in Protestant churches. He found this to be true not only in Europe but also in many segments of American Protestantism, which is virtually void of genuine sacramental piety. Even where sacraments have been faithfully observed, as in some Lutheran circles, this is often done out of a dogged obedience to the command of the Lord that we do these things, but the spontaneity of the heart has gone out of it. The sacraments then fall under the law of ritual observance, captive to the ceremonial spirit of formalism and legalism, stifling the heart of the gospel.

The rebirth of the sacraments contends not only against Protestant piety but also against the pragmatic, utilitarian bent of modern secular life. And such a rebirth, if it is genuine, should not be mistaken for a kind of romantic nostalgia for old forms of piety into which we could never really succeed in pouring the convictions of our faith. We should not minimize the odds against a genuine recovery of the sacramental principle of the gospel. Where do we find in our culture any support for the sacramental mediation of the presence of God? Do we find it in the new spirituality of mysticism? For mysticism the sacraments are at best convenient external steppingstones to inner spirituality. Like so much scaffolding, they can be kicked away once the edifice is completed; that is, the external forms can be transcended once the soul achieves an immediate relation to God. The spiritualists of the Reformation exemplified just such a superiority to the lowliness of the sacraments.

One further obstacle to the recovery of the sacramental principle of the faith in our time is that the traditional appeal to the institution of the sacraments by our Lord has become questionable in light of recent historical-critical studies. Scholars debate whether Jesus of Nazareth instituted the sacraments of baptism and the Lord's Supper in the manner in which the church has been practicing them. The specific references in the Gospels are thought by many New Testament scholars to have been words of the post-resurrection community placed in the mouth of the pre-crucifixion Jesus. At least it is no longer so unproblematic as before to base the sacraments directly on the words of the earthly Jesus. There must, in that case, be a larger christological foundation of the sacraments, one which is not reducible to the very words of the historical Jesus. The theological question is whether the sacraments make sense in terms of the whole of theology and not merely in response to explicit commands to perform them. The sacraments are meant as means of grace, as good news of the gospel embodied in concrete vessels, and not primarily as ceremonial laws to be dutifully obeyed.

Sheer obedience to dominical authority has not kept the sacraments alive in Protestant communities no matter how legalistic such communities may have been in other respects. The reason is that sacraments have lost out to a rationalistic concept of the Word of God, reducing it to revealed information about divine things, thus leaving nothing useful for sacraments to do. After all, what do they teach? How much knowledge do they convey? Do they bring about an increase of God-consciousness? For the sacraments to make sense, a totally different frame of understanding is required than in the various Protestant theologies of the Word of God, from Karl Barth to Billy Graham. The sense or non-sense of sacraments hinges on the total vision of God and his ways with the world of nature and history, with the total incarnational structure of grace and salvation in personal and communal life.

Some theologians, dissatisfied with the now questionable procedure of tracing sacraments back to a verbal institution by the historical Jesus, attempt to provide a metaphysical basis for the sacraments. They would legitimate the Christian sacraments by developing a philosophy of nature as sacramental. The term "pan-sacramentalism" refers to the notion that the whole cosmos is a sacrament. The trouble with this view is that if everything in general is a sacrament of God's presence in the world, then what is the point of sacraments in particular? If we can encounter God equally everywhere through anything, then what is the meaning of the specific sacraments which the Christian community believes to be "means of grace?" In light of the eschatological situation of salvation in Christ, it is rather the case that things of nature—words, water, bread, wine, oil—become the sacramentally representative presence of God's grace within the church and for individuals at decisive points in their lives.

A sacrament is a special synthesis of nature and history in the context of community. The three articles of the creed are united in the sacramental event. The sacraments are the indivisible actions of the Triune God in the world. A sacrament testifies to God the Creator, as we confess him in the first article of the creed, when it uses the common material and natural things of the world, signaling that all things have their origin in God and are therefore good. There are no religious, supernaturalized things that can be used, only very ordinary, untransubstantiated things like water, bread, and wine, all good enough for God to make himself present in his own creation.

A sacrament testifies to God in Jesus Christ, as we confess him in the second article of the creed, making transparently clear that God is redemptively at work in history to reclaim the fallen world as the realm of his rule. A sacrament also testifies to God the Holy Spirit, as we confess him in the third article of the creed, who heals the broken relations between human beings in this life and forms them into a true community of persons. Creator, Redeemer, Sanctifier, three personal ways in which the one God in the world and in himself work together to create a sacramental synthesis of nature, history, and community, in, with, and under which his eschatologically victorious salvation becomes really present in the world.

THE CONTROVERSY OVER THE LORD'S SUPPER

The Lutheran view of the sacramental principle has been marked by the polemical encounter between Luther and Zwingli.[2] Whatever difficulties Lutherans may have had understanding their own doctrine of the Lord's Supper, they have had no trouble distinguishing theirs from the Zwinglian-Reformed teaching. Zwingli adopted a purely symbolic view, inspired by Erasmus the humanist. The sacraments are only symbolic reminders of salvation and its spiritual blessings, and a pledge of membership in the church. They are not means by which Christ becomes truly and wholly present, really conveying the power of God's saving grace. Both Zwingli and Luther were literalists, but in different ways, and they both interpreted biblical texts symbolically, but at different places. When Luther read, "This *is* my body," he said the word "is" must be taken literally. But Zwingli took it symbolically; the *"est"* means *"significat."* When Zwingli read that Christ "ascended into heaven and sits at the right hand of the Father," he took that literally to mean that the Lord's human body is located in heaven on God's right hand, as though he were sitting in a "golden chair" beside the Father; and therefore, he cannot be bodily present in the Lord's Supper. Luther, however, interpreted the "right hand of God" symbolically to mean the omnipotent power of God by which he can be everywhere in all things, and that therefore Christ can also be present in his body in every Lord's Supper on earth no matter how many are taking place at the same time.

Zwingli explained the crass realism of passages which speak of "eating the flesh and drinking the blood of Christ" as figures of speech known as *alloeosis,* meaning "interchange"—a rhetorical device by which we may speak of divine things in human terms, of the infinite as though it were finite—whereas in reality for Zwingli the infinite and the finite belong in diametrically opposed categories.[3] Luther had an utterly different sense of the matter. What need is there to spiritualize such plain terms as "bread, wine, body, blood, eat, and drink"? Luther countered Zwingli's *alloeosis* with his doctrine of "ubiquity." Later the Reformed referred to some Lutherans as "ubiquitarians" because they followed Luther in teaching that Christ can be present in heaven and on earth and in fact everywhere, not only in his divine nature but also in his perpetually human body. Luther called Zwingli's *alloeosis* the mask of Satan, because under the guise of explaining Scripture it tears asunder what God has joined together in the incarnation, the divine and the human, destroying the truth of the gospel which irrevocably links the full revelation of God to the full humanity of Jesus. God and Jesus cannot be assigned to different planes of being and action if Jesus is forever the true identity of God revealed among us.

Luther was so adamant in his opposition to the left-wing Protestants who denied the bodily presence of Christ that by contrast he could declare himself in essential agreement with the Roman Catholic side: "For instance, we confess that in the papal church there are true holy Scriptures, true baptism, the true sacrament of the altar, the true keys to the forgiveness of sins, the true office of the ministry. . . ."[4] Luther chose three watchwords to protect the gospel from the "ravings of the rebel-lious spirits."[5] They are the sacramental union (*unio sacramentalis*), the oral manducation (*manducatio oralis*), and manducation of the unwor-thy (*manducatio indignorum*). These hard and often hated doctrines have marked the line between Lutheran and Reformed teaching. They help to account for Luther's fateful words at the Marburg Colloquy of 1529, "You are of another spirit," and for the fact that Lutherans, in spite of their problems with the pope in Rome, continue to claim close affinity with the Roman Catholic Church. "I contend," Luther said, "that in the papacy there is true Christianity, even the right kind of Christianity and many great devoted saints."[6]

What do these three watchwords mean? The idea of the sacramental union in the Lord's Supper is an excellent analogy of the hypostatic union of the two natures of Christ, the divine and the human in the one person. The bread *is* the body of Christ; the wine *is* the blood of Christ. There are three sacred prepositions in the Lutheran grammar of faith: in, with, and under. The body and blood of Christ are given *in*, *with*, and *under* the consecrated bread and wine. These prepositions will not permit us to think of the eucharistic meal as representing a vague spiritual presence of Christ, "wherever two or three are gathered together in his name." Luther could agree to this, of course, for as a matter of fact he spoke of the presence of Christ, in line with his doctrine of ubiquity, in every stone, in fire, and water, just as God is everywhere present in the world, even in the smallest leaves upon the trees. But can we find him there, just anywhere? No. We find him where he has told us to seek him and where he has promised to bind himself—to a particular loaf and a particular cup—although he is somehow present in every loaf and every cup.

In order to undergird the objective truth of the sacramental union, Luther and the Lutheran confessors stressed that the Lord's Supper is not a case of an incorporeal, spiritualized communion such as believers may enjoy any time in prayer and meditation. Instead, Christ is received through the mouth because the bread is a real participation in the body of Christ. *Manducatio oralis* means that we have only to receive Christ in our eating and drinking and not try to generate some spiritual power within ourselves by which we might be transported beyond ourselves. The basic posture at the Lord's Supper is one of radical receptivity, not spiritual activity as Zwinglian Protestants require. Since Christ puts him-self into the bread and wine, we receive him along *with* our eating and drinking. We should not imagine that we of little faith should have to go elsewhere to find Christ, to ascend on the wings of our weak faith, and commune with him spiritually, as though he were really absent from the bread and wine of which we are about to partake.

Our third watchword is *communio indignorum*—the communion of the unworthy and the impious. Luther taught that *whoever* takes the bread and the wine receives the body and blood of Christ. In the Smalcald Articles Luther made the clear statement: "Of the Sacrament of the Altar we hold that bread and wine in the Supper are the true body and blood of Christ, and are given and received not only by the godly, but also by wicked Christians."[7] The Roman Catholics could accept this, but not Zwingli and the "enthusiasts." This was Luther's "thunderbolt on the head of Dr. Karlstadt and his whole party,"[8] that not only saints but all who eat and drink, the holy and the not so holy, participate in the body of Christ. Reducing the sacrament to mere spiritual food places the burden on the subjectivity of faith to bring about communion with Christ, lifting the true believer beyond this earthly realm into heaven above. This is a challenging doctrine for spiritual athletes of Olympic stature, and extremely well-suited to the hellenistic spirituality which seeks the deities who dwell on the top of Mount Olympus.

Manducatio indignorum means that Christ is there for us prior to our believing response, and that he comes to us as one who gives himself to all, believers and unbelievers alike, in both judgment and mercy—that salvation might be absolutely free for sinners, born of grace alone, all for the sake of God's own glory.

These three watchwords are marks of classical sacramental piety. The novel doctrines of the Swiss reformers, spiritualists, enthusiasts, and their anti-sacramental Protestant epigones today threaten to destroy the earthen vessels into which God pours the gospel of his grace for the forgiveness of sins and new life in Christ. Luther professed to stand in continuity with the classical tradition of the church catholic: "The amazing thing, meanwhile, is that of all the fathers . . . not one has spoken about the sacrament as these fanatics do . . . . Actually, they simply proceed to speak as if no one doubted that Christ's body and blood are present."[9]

THE CHRISTOLOGICAL FOUNDATION OF THE LORD'S SUPPER

The sacrament of the Lord's Supper as Luther understood it was defended on two fronts. The first was an exegetical insistence on taking the words of institution literally. The second was a christological argument based on the classical doctrine of the church on the two natures and the one person of Christ. Zwingli, Calvin, Luther, and Melanchthon all agreed with the classical doctrine as it was established by the first four Ecumenical Councils from Nicaea to Chalcedon. At the Council of Chalcedon the church confessed that the union of the two natures of Christ was without division, separation, mixture, or change, while declaring that in this personal union the two natures retain their own attributes. At the same time, post-Chalcedonian standard medieval scholastic doctrine taught an exchange of attributes, the so-called *communicatio idiomatum*. Luther pounced on this doctrine and stretched it to mean that the divine attribute of omnipresence (ubiquity) was communicated to the human nature of Christ on the basis of the incarnational hypostatic union of the two natures, and therefore the whole Christ in his true body and blood can be really present on all the altars of the church at the same time. Here Luther found the christological foundation of the Lord's Supper. The whole Christ is capable of being present in the Lord's Supper, not only spiritually but really with his body and blood, because an incarnation in which the divine person is present in human form without any divine attributes would be equal to no real presence at all.

This interpretation of the *communicatio idiomatum* is called in classical Lutheran dogmatics the *genus majestaticum*. It is genuinely a "Lutheran innovation," and that is exactly what the Reformed, following Zwingli and Calvin, held against it. It went beyond the traditional scholastic interpretation of the incarnation. The Reformed party clung axiomatically to the rule, as though it were revealed from heaven, that the finite cannot contain the infinite (*finitum non capax infiniti*). The Lutherans responded to the contrary that the finite must be capable of the infinite (*finitum capax infiniti*), because that is exactly what happened in the incarnational union of God with the humanity of Jesus. The Lutherans could argue that if the human nature of Christ, because of its finitude, is incapable of the infinite, then there can be no real incarnation at all, since the divine Person of the Son of God is infinite, if he is God at all. So how can the infinite Person be present in the incarnation without the humanity of Jesus having a share in his qualities and attributes?

Luther's doctrine of the Lord's Supper required a Christology that would make it work. Otherwise Zwingli would be right, and that, as Luther so frequently said, would give us a God nobody needs and a salvation totally out of reach, unless faith has wings to fly up to heaven. But what is an incarnation for if humans have to reverse the direction and, instead of meeting God deep in human flesh, they must soar beyond the limits of finitude to encounter God at the level of the infinite? The

Lutherans suspected that the Reformed separation of the finite and the infinite was resuming the ancient Nestorian teaching of two persons in Christ, who relate to each other like two peas in a pod or like two boards glued together. That is no real union; then the work of Christ, and hence also the person, are split up. If we cannot say that God died for us, but instead, only a man, then we are lost. On account of the personal union of the natures, we can speak of the suffering of God, the blood of God, and the death of God. This is no mere verbal predication, some sort of *alloeosis*, as though its reference is merely to words in our mouth and not to works in God's history.

The quarrel between Lutherans and Reformed centered on a concept known as *extra-Calvinisticum*. For example, the Reformed Heidelberg Catechism stated: "Since the Godhead is incomprehensible and everywhere present, it must follow that it is indeed beyond the bounds of the manhood which it has assumed, and yet is nonetheless within it as well, and remains personally united to it."[10] The Lutheran position was dubbed the *infra-Lutheranum* because it held that the Son of God is totally within the flesh and never outside it (*neque logos extra carnem, neque caro extra logon*). In the incarnation God will be known in the flesh, never apart from it. Looking for God outside of his self-enfleshment struck Luther as the kind of blasphemy Christians should seek to avoid. The crucial point for Christian theology is whether God can really be taken at his word in the events of history, whether he acts in, with, and under the media of flesh and blood or whether instead the real meaning of salvation lies above history, outside of space and time. "Do not listen to those who say: 'The flesh is good for nothing.' Rather say, 'God without flesh is good for nothing.'"[11]

Although the sixteenth century ended with sharp controversies between the Lutherans and the Reformed on Christology and the Lord's Supper, driving a wedge between the two branches of the Reformation that would last for centuries, there are many healthy signs of ecumenical rapprochement in the twentieth century. Certainly we have passed beyond trench warfare into peace negotiations, as evidenced in the Leuenberg Agreements between Lutherans and Reformed in Germany. The pivotal argument between Zwingli and Luther tended to eclipse many dimensions of the Lord's Supper that have been rediscovered through biblical, patristic, liturgical, and ecumenical studies, providing a broader area of common ground than was previously thought possible. Rigid stereotypes can be broken down and new results can be expected, although they do not automatically clear away old differences that may still have far-reaching effects on worship life in our various communities. We should also remember that what panels of theologians may accomplish at the level of bilateral dialogues seldom has more than a ripple effect on the actual liturgical practice of congregations. Yet there is reason for optimism that the antithesis between the Reformed and Luther's followers can be softened, if not fully overcome.

There has been in fact a recovery of greater sacramental realism among Reformed theologians. In Germany during World War II, Christians faced an emergency situation, and in their suffering they often shared the same table of the Lord. This real fellowship in Christ has been continued and expanded in the meantime. Other factors have also played a role. There has arisen the historical-critical approach to the Bible with negative effects on the way Lutherans have traditionally argued their position on the Lord's Supper. Luther research has shown that there were real differences between Luther, Melanchthon, Chemnitz and other confessional theologians, and that these theologians by no means represent a monolithic doctrine. The ecumenical movement has opened lines of access to the traditions of Eastern Orthodoxy, widening the arena in which eucharistic theology may be developed and overcoming the frozen positions between the rival parties in Western Christianity. Altar and pulpit fellowship has been practiced between Lutherans and Reformed, convincing many believers that the Lord's Supper controversy need no longer divide the communions.

The critical study of the Scriptures has made it clear that neither Luther nor the Lutheran tradition grasped the *totality* of the biblical witness to the Lord's Supper. They point us to essential aspects, but we do not possess in our Lutheran tradition a complete theology of the Lord's Supper. Some Lutheran theologians today believe that in the heat of the Reformation polemics against the medieval concept of the sacrifice in the Mass, the baby was thrown out with the bath. There has been an attempt to restore the motif of sacrifice to the Sacrament of the Altar, but not in its medieval sense. There can be, of course, no question of a repetition of the sacrifice on Golgotha in the Eucharist; rather, the once-for-all sacrifice on the cross is re-presented again and again in the church. The various Christian communions can agree to this, properly understood.

Lutherans in the ecumenical movement have not been pressured to abandon their historic stress on the real presence. Luther's sacramental realism has been vindicated by contemporary inquiries into the New Testament, especially into John and Paul. However, as the Eastern Orthodox theologians have pointed out, Lutherans have tied the real presence too exclusively to the elements. The late medieval discussions became bogged down in categories of Aristotelian substance metaphysics; today we are free to use new conceptual tools to speak of the real presence of the whole Christ. Every shift in Christology will reflect itself in sacramental doctrine. And these shifts now cut across denominational lines. Lutherans are free to entertain any new conceptual system that may help to speak realistically of the presence of Christ in Holy Communion, and they are required by their confessional stance to be critical of every system that undermines the sacramental principle of the gospel.

There are other motifs that demand their due in sacramental theology today. Biblical theology has recovered for us a sense of the eschatological dimension of the early church's celebration of the Supper. It was a meal of joy and anticipation. The image of the church as the body of Christ helps to offset Protestant individualism. The memorial aspect, "This do in remembrance of me," needs to be stressed, for it is now clear that Zwingli's rationalistic interpretation of the idea of "anamnesis" does not do justice to its biblical meaning. "Anamnesis" is not merely a mental recollection of something or someone past and now absent. It is rather a re-calling and re-presenting of "an event in the past so that it becomes living, powerful and operative."[12] Those Protestants who traditionally honor the memorial feature of the meal can be helped to appreciate a richer realism implied in the biblical motif of remembrance.

THE CONTEMPORARY CRISIS IN CHRISTOLOGY

The sixteenth-century debate between Lutherans and Reformed on the relation between finite and infinite centered on an issue that still plays an important role in the contemporary crisis in Christology. The debate surrounding *The Myth of God Incarnate*[13] is a case study of what happens in Christian theology when the infinity of God is defined as metaphysically incapable of expressing itself in a revelationally and soteriologically definitive way in the one finite particular event of Jesus Christ. The contributors to this popular volume of essays make some assertions that show them to be hooked on a metaphysical *a priori* that links them specifically to the Reformed principle, *finitum non capax infiniti.*

Maurice Wiles, for example, asks whether the very concept of an incarnate being who is both fully God and fully man is really intelligible. Of course not because, after all, the finite is incapable of the infinite.[14] Frances Young is troubled about what she calls a "literal incarnation" because she finds it intellectually impossible to make the ontological equation: Jesus equals God.[15] Of course not because, after all, there can be no ontologically real incarnation and hypostatic union of God in his personal essence and human nature. She wants to spell out the relation between God and Jesus along other than incarnational lines. She even resorts to the ninteenth-century notion of *als ob* used in Kantian and Ritschlian circles. Lacking the ontological equation of Jesus with God, the only way to retain the liturgical symbols of the Christian tradition is to continue to speak of Jesus Christ "as if he were God for us"[16]— Zwingli's *alloeosis* warmed over for modern consumption.

Michael Goulder would set aside the Nicene idea of *homoousios* in favor of *homopraxis*,[17] preferring thereby a Christology of agency to one of substance. Goulder concludes his essay with these outrageous words: "The incarnational speculations introduced into the church by Simon Magus and his fellow-Samaritans seem to me entirely dispensable."[18] Don Cupitt likewise minces no words: the classical Christian doctrine of the incarnation does not belong to the essence of Christianity but remains bound to an obsolete portion of church history.[19] John Hick, the editor of this volume of christological essays, tries to explain how Jesus of Nazareth came to be deified in ancient Christianity through a shift of image from Son of God to God the Son,[20] and that is a move we modern-day Christians no longer need to make and, indeed, ought not make in a world seeking to expand harmony among the great religions of the world.[21] For no doubt traditional trinitarian and christological ideas reinforce the exclusivistic kerygmatic line that Christianity derived from the New Testament.

The dyscarnational Christology of this book of essays breaks the linkage between the identity and reality of God and the person and history of Jesus. Why does it do that? The reason is clear in light of the old motto: *finitum non capax infiniti*. The writers have implicitly, perhaps unwittingly, bought into the *extra-Calvinisticum*. Extra means "outside of." They have access to the true saving knowledge of God *outside of* his self-definition in the person of Jesus, that is, *extra carnem Christi*. The Logos of John's Gospel is not totally embodied within the flesh but freely roams the universe with only an accidental, incidental connection to the history of Jesus.

Luther once said that the author of the Fourth Gospel was not a Platonist but an evangelist. The metaphysical presupposition of these authors is clearly Platonist or Neoplatonist. Their underlying difficulty with the incarnational union of infinite and finite is the graceless and faceless absolute of Hellenistic metaphysics, which found it ontologically impossible to live and move and have its being in history, in human form, in a state of humiliation. The metaphysical absolute of Hellenistic philosophy would not be caught dead in the person of Jesus and his destiny on the cross. But what if God is not a prisoner of such a metaphysical straitjacket? Luther said that God reveals himself *sub contrario.* The infinite is capable of the finite; it happened in the incarnation. This is not metaphysical nonsense but dialectical truth, that the infinite would mediate itself through the finite. And so the timeless metaphysics of Hellenistic philosophy must be revised on the basis of a thoroughgoing historical hermeneutics of biblical revelation. Then the story of Jesus is the key to God's autobiography. Frances Young says that she is not prepared to suggest "that something happened in 'God's biography' when Jesus died on the cross."[22] So what God is she talking about? The God of the gospel is capable of an intrinsic openness to the identity, attributes, and experiences of human existence in the world, and this is neither conceptually unintelligible nor ontologically impossible.

This journey into the labyrinth of ancient christological categories has been necessary to show that the sacramental principle lives in the medium of a whole christological vision of the way in which God approaches us *in, with,* and *under* forms of finitude, paradigmatically in the hypostatic union of the incarnation and analogically in the sacramental union of the Lord's Supper.

A SACRAMENTAL VISION OF THE CREATION

The incarnational foundation of sacramental presence has connections with the whole of life. The holiness of God appears in human form, and his infinite transcendence arrives within the material matrix of creation. Because of the real humanity of God in Christ, the wall of separation between the holy and the common, the religious and the secular, the soul and the body, this world and the one to come, history and eschatology, the natural and the supernatural has been broken down. In the history of the church the wall has been erected again and again, and the new community in Christ has lapsed back into a basically Jewish conception of holiness. "For the Jews, the holy was that which was set apart from the ordinary uses of the world, that which was not common. Indeed, the 'common' was equated with the 'unclean,' the very antithesis of the 'holy'."[23] The Christian view which derives from the incarnation is that the holy becomes common, even commonplace. Holy transcendence becomes lowly immanence. The familiar, ordinary, common, run-of-the-mill things of this world take on special significance when the real presence is manifest not in specially holy things but in the vital universe of material things. In the sacramental vision there is nothing the matter with matter. As C. S. Lewis aptly said, "God likes matter; he invented it." The cocoon of religion, wrapped up in its own ceremonies, could not hold Jesus Christ, and he summons his followers into the world to breathe the fresh air of God's creation, not stay closeted up inhaling the holy smoke of stuffy religious ceremonies. The sacraments of the real presence dramatize the bold and holy secularity expressed in the Christian doctrines of creation, incarnation, and sanctification.

As we have said, the sacrament of the body and blood of Christ has a deep set of roots in the soil of the Incarnation, but it has another set of roots deeply embedded in the Christian doctrine of creation. For the body of Christ is continuous with the created body of humanity, being "like unto us in every respect, except without sin." There is continuity between creation and incarnation, and so it is fitting that the sacrament of salvation should use as its means of expression the same earthly kind of stuff from which humanity emerged in its evolutionary journey. The biblical basis for stressing humanity's continuity with the good earth is classically expressed in Gen. 3:19: "In the sweat of your face you shall eat bread till you return to the ground, for out of it you were taken; you are dust and to dust you shall return." On account of the influence of Gnosticism, Christian doctrine has tended to neglect the earthly medium of the creation of humanity. Human life is not external to the earth but one of its vital forms. The earthly environment gives us the bread we need to live, so the earth is always "mother earth" and at the same time womb, home, and grave for humanity.

There was a heretic in the early church, Carpocrates, who under the influence of Gnosticism defined the soul in radical distinction from the body, the one being spiritual and infinite, the other material and finite. So the Carpocratians cultivated the higher spiritual values of the soul. Since the body was good for nothing, hopelessly corrupt, they indulged its desires and used it in shameful ways. Their motto was: "To the pure, all things are pure." St. Irenaeus wrote that the Carpocratians practiced the principle: "Give to the flesh the things of the flesh and to the spirit the things of the spirit." They separated what God joined together, body and soul, in one personal life.

A sacramental vision of life reacts positively to the contemporary search for an ecologically sound theology and ethic. The concept of the "whole person" and the "whole earth" are building blocks of such a theology. Human life cannot be whole without the whole earth. When the earth becomes polluted, people become sick. As humans we enjoy a symbiotic relationship with all the natural elements of the earth. Without their B vitamins, which come from the earth, human beings become insane. *Sanus* in Latin means "sound" or "whole." The Christian tradition has often one-sidedly stressed the other side of wholeness, the spiritual need of grace and the forgiveness of sins to become whole. That is a truth from which we would not wish to retreat in trying to rectify the imbalance that has crept into spiritualizing trends in Christianity. When Christian theology has dealt with the salvation drama in history—creation and fall, sin and guilt, cross and resurrection, the church and the consummation—it has often left the body behind as so much excess baggage. But in the biblical vision salvation is holistic; healing is not a partial process that affects only the "soul." The vision is all-embracing; the earth goes together with heaven, and the body with soul. What happens in our human bodies has repercussions on the spiritual dimension of life. Therefore, when humans destroy the balance of nature, not only soil, plants, and animals are affected, but the human body pays the highest price.

The modern liturgical movement has stressed the connections between liturgy and life. We are going one step farther in tracing connections between the sacramental and the somatic aspects of life. Christian theology has seldom retained the full somatic potential of its own inherent incarnational spirituality. It has excelled in probing the depths of subjectivity, interiority, individuality, and personality, often neglecting the somatic foundations of life and all too often allowing "reverence for life" (Schweitzer)—respect for the body and care of the earth—to evaporate into abstractions. Western philosophy betrays a similar profound neglect of the materialistic origins and conditions of human life, exhibiting a prejudice against nature. If we examine the record, we see a philosophy of ideas in Plato, a philosophy of consciousness in Descartes, a philosophy of existence in Heidegger, and a philosophy of language in Wittgenstein, while the bodily basis of thought and theory has been neglected. And Buber's "I-thou" relationship is a pure abstraction without the bodies of flesh and blood that bump against each other. One is reminded of the saying of Plotinus (a Neoplatonist philosopher): "The true philosopher is entirely concerned with the soul and not the body. He would like, as far as he can, to get away from the body . . . to dissever the soul from the communion of the body."[24]

Christianity veered into spiritualism under the impact of Hellenization and at the same time mishandled its Jewish sources. So Ludwig Feuerbach could charge: "With Christianity man lost the capability of conceiving himself as a part of Nature, of the universe."[25] Although Israel was caught in a horrendous struggle between Baal, the god of fertility, and Yahweh, the God of history, condemning the idolatry in the religion of fertility, still the festivals of nature were not excluded from the history of God with his people. There were the festivals of unleavened bread, of weeks, and of the fruit harvest. These brought joy to the people of Israel, and through them they praised God for the good earth, its yield of grain and oil and fruit. What Israel achieved was to make the God of fertility subject to Yahweh, the Lord of history, so that the people were liberated from the worship of earth and body. But in entering history, Israel did not abandon nature. Israel continued to have holy places—Shechem, Shiloh, Gilgal, and Jerusalem—not just holy seasons and holy times. Israel did not sever its connection with the earth. The promise from which Israel lived included hope for a good land flowing with milk and honey and, in Israel's later post-exilic period, for the resurrection of the body, a new heaven and a new earth.

Israel's down-to-earth spirituality prepared the way for the full-bodied sacramental principle in Christian faith and life. We must remember that New Testament sacraments run the risk of losing their earthward connections without the Old Testament witness to the whole creation as the context of covenant history. We can find elements of this witness by looking first at the hymns of creation and second at the hymns of judgment. In Psalm 104, for example, the poet depicts the world—vegetative, animal, and human—as God's creation. God's breath is the life principle of all things. The hymns of judgment arise in face of the evil deeds of humanity. People damage and destroy the creation of God, including themselves. They do not care for the earth, so the earth mourns and languishes by the violence of men (Hos. 4:3). Heaven and earth are called to witness against humanity; they have heard the oaths of allegiance to the Creator; and they have suffered the full force of human violence. If we read the Old Testament with eyes renewed by ecological sensitivity today, we will see things to which we were blind before. Walter Harrelson writes that these Old Testament testimonies "have something to say about a world corrupted by nuclear explosions, a world stripped of its beauty by greed, a world raped by exploiters of its treasures, an earth that will not be permitted to yield its treasures for the indiscriminate good of all but must become the habitation of helpless, indolent men incapable of work. In short, a bruised and desecrated earth cries out against its violators."[26] Israel's vision of humanity and its earthly environment can inspire in us a new vision of the beauty of the earth made whole, a vision in which union with God in the sphere of the sacramental includes our commonality with the whole creation. Luther picked up this notion of human solidarity with the whole creation in his explanation of the First Article of the Apostles' Creed: "I believe that God has created me and all that exists."

IMPLICATIONS FOR LIFE TODAY

Nothing better concretizes our human interconnection with the earth than the foods we eat. The well-known saying of a German philosopher makes the point: *Man ist was man isst.* "We are what we eat." This may remind us of the materialistic component in the Christian belief system. Both the doctrine of creation and that of the Incarnation make the matter of the earth the medium of the creative Word and Spirit, which Irenaeus called the "two hands of God." We have insisted in this chapter on the importance of the Lutheran prepositions *in, with,* and *under* as expressive of the sacramental principle. Now we wish to extend this principle into various spheres of life today.

Organic matter becomes food for life. In addition to food, we require air and water from the environment. Breathing clean air and drinking pure water are as necessary as eating healthy food. In the Bible we do not find a metaphysics of food as in some Eastern religions, but we do find a symbolics of food, most concentrated in the sacrament of eating and drinking. In early Christian life eating and drinking were considered religious acts, there having been as yet no dichotomy between the religious and the secular. The simple act of offering a prayer before and after the meal is a vestige of this religious view of eating and drinking. Many of us were brought up in a daily practice that kept family, food, and faith together. Compare that to the secularized style in America today. People rush in from the streets, do not quiet their bodies through any ritual pause, gulp down some instant foods, and return to the same stressful situations which jangle the nerves. The communal meaning of eating and drinking has vanished—communion with the sources of life, with family and friends, and with the Lord who is present as the host of every sacramental action.

One early Christian writer glimpsed a close connection between eating and drinking with Jesus in Holy Communion and the bread which every person needs simply to exist. "When we come together to break bread, we must break it to the hungry, to God himself in his poor members."[27] This writer was harking back to Paul's letter to the Corinthians, who were eating and drinking damnation to themselves because the rich members were ignoring the poor in their midst, and who kept food for themselves which was to be shared with the poor and needy. For by eating up the food beforehand, they showed they had no sense of the body of Christ present in all the members. In some way the presence of God is associated with eating and drinking, not only in the Lord's Supper but in every meal. In Protestantism there has been a progressive tendency to desacralize both liturgy and life, with the result that eating and drinking become mere secular activities, without ritual and sacred meaning. The spiritualization of the sacrament leads to the secularization of ordinary eating, with the next step being the denaturalization of food to the benefit of today's greedy counterfeiters in the food industry who sell chemicalized, cancer-producing food and drink for unconscionable profits. The ecology movement includes a small but dedicated consumer revolt against plastic and poison foods in favor of natural and organic foods. At first the large food companies regarded this movement as subversive and mounted a massive campaign against so-called health foods with the aid of their favorite medical authorities, but more recently they have begun to coopt the movement by deceptively labeling their own products with the magic words "natural" and "whole" and "organic."

The "whole person" movement is based on a vision of the psychosomatic unity of the human being. This calls for therapy of the whole person, a new kind of health service now called "holistic." The governing idea of salvation and healing is holistic. Health is wholeness based on the message that God was in Christ, a whole human person (*totus homo*), who came to bring life and salvation, to make people whole, to heal the sick, to be for every person the Great Physician, the master-model of what it means to care for others. Paul Tournier, a medical doctor and lay theologian, has said, "Medicine has lost the sense of the person, the sense of man as a whole."[28] This vision of the whole person is nurtured by the sacramental life of the church and must join the struggle to reform the systems in our society that are meant to care for the sick and the dying, to fight disease and promote health. God help the sick person who falls into the hands of specialists who take a piecemeal approach to the person.

The church operates hospitals and supports chaplains out of a correct sense that a person is more than a collection of parts, more than a system of physical functions, and more than a body of feelings and emotions. There is a personal center which we call "spirit," the central unity of the physical, mental, and emotional aspects of life. The spirit is the self that can say "I." We must deal with a person as a whole—body, mind, and soul—and spirit is the name of that whole, the center of the self which lives in, with, and under all its different dimensions.

The sacramental vision we have lifted up is in search of a vital ethic in the struggles of our day. Religious vision and ethical motivation are basic ingredients of a radical alternative to the hell-bent course of things today. They must play a part in a new construction of humanity. Christian faith has an inner commitment to fight against the forces that lead to decay, degeneration, and death. Ours is a message of life, hope for new possibilities, and solidarity with every positive trend that promotes human welfare and development. There is nothing in the Christian message that ties us fatalistically to the barbaric forces at loose in the conflicts of this nuclear age, which threaten to inflict omnicide on both humanity and the earth in the name of peoples' liberation, democratic values, technological progress, scientific theory, economic growth, and such ideologically distorted slogans.

Christianity ought to stress anew that it is a religion of salvation for humanity and the world. Its primary calling is to proclaim salvation and to bring the forces of healing to bear upon the whole person and the whole earth. The New Testament definition of the Christian calling is: "Heal the sick; cast out demons." Today that means also the healing of the biosphere and driving out all the powers that make the earth foul and filthy. Salvation and health cannot be split. The reception of salvation means the chance to become sane and sound and whole in all dimensions of one's being. Jesus is the Great Physician because he possesses power to heal the whole person. He is Healer and Savior, but not in the sense of salvaging some weightless and soulish substance. He is Healer and Savior because he does not cut off any part of life or suppress it. He is the announcer and bringer of a new reality that makes us hope and work for the conversion and transformation of the old. This promise of new reality is what keeps us from surrendering to despair in the midst of this dying world. For in Christ the kindgom of God has appeared, and its nature is salvation—healing of all that is ill, making all things whole.

NOTES

1. An excellent example is the recent work of Geoffrey Wainwright, *Doxology: The Praise of God in Worship, Doctrine, and Life* (New York: Oxford University Press, 1980).

2. Hermann Sasse, *This is My Body: Luther's Contention for the Real Presence in the Sacrament of the Altar* (Minneapolis: Augsburg Publishing House, 1959).

3. Ibid., pp. 150 ff.

4. "Concerning Rebaptism (1528)," *LW* 40:231.

5. Ibid., p. 232.

6. Ibid.

7. The Smalcald Articles (1537), III, vi, in *The Book of Concord*, trans. and ed. Theodore G. Tappert (Philadelphia: Fortress Press, 1959), p. 311.

8. "Against the Heavenly Prophets (1525)," *LW* 40:177.

9. "This is My Body (1527)," *LW* 37:54.

10. *Heidelberg Catechism*, Question 48.

11. Theodosius Harnack, *Luthers Theologie*, (Erlangen: Theodor Blaesing, 1927), 2nd ed., 2:105.

12. Neville Clark, *An Approach to the Theology of the Sacraments* (London: SCM Press, 1956), p. 62.

13. John Hick, ed., *The Myth of God Incarnate* (Philadelphia: Westminster Press, 1977).

14. Ibid., p. 5.

15. Ibid., p. 35.

16. Ibid., p. 39.

17. Ibid., p. 62.

18. Ibid., p. 85.

19. Ibid., p. 134.

20. Ibid., p. 175.

21. The challenge of the religious pluralism today has shocked many Western theologians out of their christological wits. In order to open channels of reasonable dialogue, some have found it psychologically imperative to abandon the central affirmations of classical Christology.

22. John Hick, *Myth of God Incarnate*, p. 47, n. 49.

23. John A. T. Robinson, *Liturgy Coming to Life* (London: A. R. Mowbray, 1960), p. 39.

24. Quoted by D. Owen, *Body and Soul* (Philadelphia: Westminster Press, 1956), p. 39.

25. Ludwig Feuerbach, *The Essence of Christianity*, trans. George Eliot (New York: Harper & Brothers, 1957), p. 133.

26. Walter Harrelson, *From Fertility Cult to Worship* (Garden City, N.Y.: Doubleday & Co., 1970), p. 74.

27. John A. T. Robinson, *On Being the Church in the World* (London: SCM Press, 1960), p. 68.

28. Paul Tournier, *The Whole Person in a Broken World* (New York: Harper & Row, 1964), p. 38.

6 The Law/Gospel Principle

WHAT IS THE GOSPEL?

Four hundred years ago, in 1576, Martin Chemnitz's classic *Examination of the Council of Trent* was translated from Latin and printed in German.[1] I returned to it recently to refresh my memory on how sixteenth-century Lutherans understood the gospel of Jesus Christ differently from the Roman bishops at the Council of Trent. Martin Chemnitz spoke lucidly of the *krinomenon*[2]—the real point of difference concerning the article of justification through faith alone. Chemnitz stands third behind Luther and Melanchthon in giving shape and direction to the theology of the Lutheran movement. With respect to the gospel of justification *sola fide*, no theologian has written with greater precision concerning what is the real issue in this article of faith. It is not a fight over words among squabbling theologians but a dealing with matters that determine the standing of every person before God.

There are numerous signs that *gospel* is a word with a very vague meaning in modern usage. We are treated to everything from the *Gospel According to Peanuts* to the *Gospel According to the Wall Street Journal*. In liberation theology the "gospel" represents the ideal state of affairs, which hopefully will come about some day and for which we ought to fight with all our might and main. The gospel is captured by ideology. We hear about the *demands* of the gospel which prescribe for Christians the kind of liberating praxis to which they ought to commit themselves. The future kingdom comes about through a synergism of divine grace and good works, in this case the right kind of political praxis. The notes of *sola gratia* and *sola fide* are simply not to be found in the score played by the liberation theologians. This lack of the *grace* note came home to me one day in a seminar on liberation theology. Analyzing a text of Gustavo Gutierrez, the class came upon a passage in which the author was criticizing the attempt of the church to proclaim a bond of unity in spite of the class conflict between rich and poor.[3] The idea of a unity between rich and poor in the midst of class conflict only puts the church on the side of the oppressor class. The idea of unity is a myth, which does nothing to resolve the tensions between class enemies. The church must come to the side of the oppressed class, offering the ideal of unity as a goal which will be achieved only when the division between rich and poor is overcome. What then is the gospel *prior to* the end of the class conflict? Is it only a goad to action, or is it a real presence of the goal in the midst of the conflictive situation? Will the gospel become true when we reach the goal of unity, or is it already real in spite of the gap between the promises of God and the facts of history? Is there a real presence of the gospel before the arrival of the final kingdom? This was the most internationally pluralistic and ecumenically representative class I have ever taught, and it broke up in a heated discussion concerning "What is the gospel?" in the midst of the liberation struggles of our day.

The idea that as the church we can already celebrate and practice a unity of humanity in Christ—that in Christ there is no East or West, no rich or poor, no slave or free, no male or female, no Jew or Greek, no black or white, no Brahman or pariah, no prince or pauper—is seemingly dismissed as a myth contrary to the facts of human existence. Such a vision of unity and universality, desirable as it may be, is a task that lies before us; it is not a gift which we can already share as a datum of eschatological salvation prior to its world-historical actualization and in spite of the ambiguities of present social reality. Thus, we witness a modern variant of works righteousness, not on the individualistic model of late medieval piety but on the political model of modern revolutionary theory. Eschatology is reduced to ethics. The kingdom of God arrives as a result of the ethical achievements of humanity. The gospel of the kingdom of God is removed to the future as a goal to be attained by the right kind of ethical activity. The gospel is not received as a present reality in history, already prior to human action, in the person and ministry of Jesus Christ. The gospel has become law!

Neither the Formula of Concord nor Martin Chemnitz used the language of history and eschatology in speaking of the gospel and eternal life. But the point of difference—the *krinomenon*—is equally applicable whether we speak of the gospel of justification or the gospel of the kingdom of God vis à vis the sum total of human ethical works of righteousness. Neither the works of personal righteousness nor the works of political righteousness can build a staircase for approaching the kingdom of God or eternal life.

Martin Chemnitz made the paradox of justification ever so clear that it is sinners who are justified before God, prior to any change for the better in their sinful condition and in spite of the fact that they can point to no inherent quality that puts them in the situation of grace. The gospel of justification does not stand upon our virtues, change of heart, or good works. The gospel is not a word for a movement going on within our subjectivity. The difference, therefore, between transactional analysis or transcendental meditation and the gospel is as great as that between night and day. It is truly liberating to know that there is simply nothing in us, whether we are Christians or just plain pagans, by which we can be justified before God. Yet justification happens—received through faith alone and solely on account of Christ.

I am persuaded that Chemnitz's formulation of the *krinomenon* was not a polemical statement limited in relevance to the extreme synergism of Andrada the Jesuit and other papal theologians. Even if the word *justification* is no longer the main theme of any contemporary theology, we are still dealing with the substantive issue of how we stand as individuals and groups before God. Even if we speak of eschatological salvation or the kingdom of God, we are still faced with the question of what it is to which we can point which promises grace, what we can rely on in the ultimate judgment, what will relieve the bitter accusations of conscience, who can make enemies become friends, who can convert a heart of stone, who can offer the assurance of eternal life. Jesus Christ is Chemnitz's answer to these questions. The important point in this answer—the *krinomenon*—is that the verdict of justification is valid *prior to* the works of the regenerate heart and *in spite of* every human failure. Any qualification of this priority and this paradox leads to synergistic heresy and the legalization of the gospel. Holding fast to the message of justification in all its stark forensic priority offers, furthermore, the only sure guarantee against boasting in ourselves, that all our boasting may be in the Lord by whom Christ has been made our righteousness (1 Cor. 1:30).

It is possible to reconstruct a picture of what the gospel meant to the confessing fathers of the Lutheran Reformation. We can study the phenomenon of the gospel as the word appears in its many language contexts in *The Book of Concord*, in Luther's own writings, as well as in the works of Melanchthon and Chemnitz. Here we are going to draw a picture of the phenomenon to which we are committed as heirs of the Reformation and its confessional documents. We do this not only to show where we have come from as a testimony about our origins, but where we are now as a confession of our inmost identity.

1. In a time when some Lutherans are still embroiled in a controversy over the Bible, it seems important to remind ourselves that the gospel is not another word for Scripture. The inner goal of the gospel is to be proclaimed in a living voice. Someone has quoted Luther as calling the gospel "an acoustical affair." It is an appropriate expression whether one can find it in Luther or not.

2. The gospel is not a system of universal truths about divine subjects which one can deduce from Scripture and collect in a volume of dogmatics. Rather, it is the living Word of God to me. Until I have heard this Word in existential inwardness, I have heard nothing of the gospel. Until I can say, this is *for me*—God has created *me* and all that exists; he has redeemed *me*, a lost and condemned creature; he has called *me* through the gospel—I have not grasped the personal dimension of the gospel, which is the epistemological point of access to every other dimension, social as well as cosmic. Individualism has become a bad word. It points to a massive restriction of the gospel to the inner life of the private person. Liberation theology has brought this charge against existentialist Christianity. Existentialism in turn is rooted in pietism, which has influenced almost every Lutheran in America. Yet there is an undeniable element of egoism in salvation. There is an individual thrust and focus of the gospel, as it puts the spotlight on me as a regenerate rebel, sinner, and saint at the same time before God *(simul iustus et peccator).*

3. The existential focus of the gospel is no excuse for letting it slide into the slush of subjectivism. For the gospel which is heard is not grounded in me, but in Christ outside of me. The *pro me* of the gospel is based on God's act in Christ. Away with individualism, but not with the personalizing thrust of the gospel! Perhaps nothing in our times has done more to captivate the preaching of the gospel than the amateur psychologizing which plays peekaboo from the pulpit with people's personal problems, whereas the *Christus extra nos* and *pro nobis* alone can make the preacher's talk into gospel speech. Chemnitz referred to his opponents who, playing tricks with words, leave aside the announcement of God's justifying act in Christ as *logodaidaloi*—"wordsmiths."[4] Preachers become professional *logodaidaloi* when their words fail to frame the picture of Jesus Christ as God's way of justifying the world.

In *The Book of Concord* the word *gospel* is used sometimes in a larger sense as the whole Word of God to be found in the Holy Scriptures, and sometimes in the strict sense of the promise of the forgiveness of sins. The gospel is a promise. But it is not a conditional promise in the synergistic sense that I promise to do something in the future, if only you will first do your part. The gospel is not only a promise of future hope, but also a proclamation of present grace. The gospel tells us that God both makes and keeps his promises—for us and for Christ's sake alone.

LAW AND GOSPEL

A theology of the gospel can be developed, according to our confessions, only within a cluster of supporting concepts. A common error in understanding the gospel is to isolate it from the entire sweep of reality from beginning to end. We usually fail to reach far enough back or far enough forward, so to speak. We restrict the gospel, perhaps, to the person and work of Christ and assign to him a role in the realm of personal redemption; thus we lose his intrinsic connection with the creation of the world, the covenant with Israel, the mission of the church, and the future of the cosmos. The gospel reaches backwards and forward all along the line from creation to consummation because Christ is the eschatological revelation of God already at the beginning of things. The world was created through Christ, and all things will ultimately reach their end in him as Judge and Lord. This is the biblical meaning of calling Christ the *alpha* and the *omega*. I believe our confessions presuppose this backward and forward extension of Christ, but there is obviously no full development and elaboration of the significance of Christ for the whole process of the world and history from beginning to end. The Lutheran confessions deal with the central content of the gospel as it bears on personal salvation, which is the point at which the controversy with Rome erupted.

But if the confessions do not go far enough back to develop the fuller connections of the gospel with the totality of reality, they do reach back to the law as a fundamental presupposition of the gospel. The gospel is not the Word of God apart from the law. Each has a different function. The law of God meets every person somehow through the Scriptures, conscience, and the natural orders of life in history and society. One synodical bishop wrote to one of his pastors: "Don't preach anything controversial." Little did he realize that he was pulling the plug on the gospel. The law is God's controversy with his people. The law terrifies, accuses, condemns, denounces, punishes, and kills. If this is not true, then the gospel cannot comfort, strengthen, forgive, liberate, and renew. In the religious life, law and gospel are correlative. In addition to this religious use of the law, there is the political use, the function of law within the public domain. Here its purpose is to order society, to prevent chaos, and to punish crime. Lutherans have been sensitive to both functions of the law.

If preaching is sick today, it is because we do not know how to preach the law. We are lulling people to sleep with the gospel when they should be roused by means of the law. August Tholuck, preacher and theologian in Germany in the last century, said: "If by any chance a peddler of indulgences were to appear among us, he would not do a good business; for nobody has a disquieted and alarmed conscience."[5] People are not looking for a gracious God but a good deal, and preachers are helping them. According to the confessions, other alienating concepts must be introduced to make the gospel *qua* gospel stand out. Not only the law but such positively negative symbols as sin and Satan, wrath and hell, in whatever modern idiom, must be preached to put starch into the gospel. The twin process of demythologizing and psychologizing has ferreted these negative terms out of usage in most preaching today. We do not know how to speak of the realities to which they point. But this we can say: if the gospel is not placed in bold relief against the background of the demonic, sin, wrath and hell, it degenerates into a saccharine-sweet message of civilizing aphorisms. When Jesus Christ is pictured in the confessional writings, he is the fulfiller of the law, the appeaser of wrath, the victor over Satan, the conqueror of death, the atoner of sin— all concepts which have suffered an erosion of meaning in our monistic universe of discourse.

The law tells us what we ought to do; the gospel declares what God does. The law demands and threatens; the gospel gives and forgives. But when a person hears the "thunder of Sinai," several things can happen. The law can aggravate a person's rebellion, like a child whose hatred of his or her father increases with every lash of the whip. Or the law can be taken seriously as a way of salvation and thus lead to the righteousness of works. The law says you ought to be righteous. It is reasonable to assume, Kant said, that if you ought, you can. That was also the reasoning of Erasmus against Luther and, before that, Pelagius against Augustine. The "natural man" is a born Pelagian. We hear the law and use it as an occasion of pride, illusion, and self-righteousness. But the law does more: it drives the self-reliant person into despair. It pulls the props out from under a person; it casts him or her into the slough of despondency, self-accusation, anxiety, and suicide. Thus the law prepares the way for the hearing of the good news of divine grace freely offered.

But even after the reception of forgiveness, the law enters as a threat. It tries to legalize the gospel. This happens when preachers announce: "You are saved by grace, but . . . ." Grace is not grace if there are any ifs, ands, or buts about it. Grace is unconditional. There is no salvation based on works. The sinner is incapable of doing God-pleasing works. For the

Christian it is nothing less than a blasphemy to tie salvation to one's own good works, for that detracts from the sufficiency of Christ and leads to boasting. If grace is conditional, the church might as well go into the business of offering green stamps. This is actually what the radio and TV evangelists have learned to do even more effectively than John Tetzel.

The Lutheran confessions are clear about this: whatever is not of faith is sin. The law cannot produce faith, and the works of the law cannot lead to a liberated life of grace. Therefore, the confessions insist so vigorously on the *sola fide*. The classic formula is *iustificatio propter Christum per fidem*. But this formula is itself capable of falsification. The confessions speak often of "justifying faith." They say that "faith alone justifies" and "faith alone is counted as our righteousness." Under these phrases the old ghost of synergism may be permitted to hide. But in fact there is no problem if we understand faith as a miracle of grace, not as a human possibility. The Apology to the Augsburg Confession says, "Faith does not justify or save because it is a good work in itself." John Calvin also saw the possibility of importing the old synergism under the slogan of faith. So he said, *"La foi ne justifie pas entant que c'est une oeuvre que nous faisons."*[6] To be sure, faith is a good work, but it is the good work of the Spirit. Faith alone means Christ alone, for faith is the awareness worked by the Spirit that salvation is not from us, but for us. Faith is not the response of a person's free will to choose the grace of God. The confessions slam the door on free will to keep out every possible synergistic intrusion. They reject the statement used by some of the ancient Fathers that God draws, but draws the person who is willing. Instead, God makes unwilling persons willing to do the will of Christ. All is of grace that nothing shall be of works, not even the work of believing the true doctrines of the faith. The ladders of free will, reason, and religious emotion are all stripped away so that faith may stick to the ground of God's grace in the earthly Christ.

Yet all this confessional clarity on grace and faith did not succeed in preventing pharisaism from reappearing in Lutheranism under the cloak of pietism.

THE *ORDO SALUTIS*

The forensic act of declaring the sinner *just* makes the sinner just indeed in the sight of God. Regeneration and new obedience result from the justifying work of God. The priority of justification does not imply a neglect of regeneration. Likewise, the primacy of faith does not entail a neglect of works. An emphasis on the Christ *for us* does not negate the reality of the Christ *within us.* There is a mystical union of the believer with Christ, but always on the basis of the objective Christ outside us.

The confessions are not a systematic theology. They make no systematic effort to develop in serial fashion all the psychological interconnections of various concepts in the whole process of salvation. There is no logical, chronological, or psychological spelling out of an ordered sequence of experience. There is, in short, no developed *ordo salutis* in the confessions as we find later in the periods of orthodoxy and pietism. Concepts like reconciliation, propitiation, righteousness, justification, redemption, satisfaction, renovation, renewal, regeneration, sanctification, and the like are not all elaborated seriatim. Later orthodoxy must have regarded this as a deficiency because the seventeenth-century theologians tried to work out the way of salvation in a sequence of concepts that presumably correspond to the logic of experience.

Biblical theology today would affirm the confessional pattern more than the orthodox-pietistic *ordo salutis*, looking at the biblical terms for salvation as word pictures depicting the grace event in Christ as one indivisible whole, simply to be received through faith. The word pictures are more like spokes on a wheel than links in a chain. By the same token, there is no biblical warrant to single out the word *justification* as the prime soteriological category nor to restrict its meaning to its strictly forensic aspect of imputation. Yet this term has the merit of highlighting that salvation is by grace alone, that it presupposes nothing meritorious in the human condition, and that its validity depends on Christ alone, not on any change for the better in us.

If the gospel means the forgiveness of sins apart from the works of the law, engendering a response of faith and love, why do the confessions include the doctrine of election in their theology of the gospel? In the Solid Declaration XI, we read that everything "concerning our redemption, call, justification, and salvation" is, "according to the Scriptures . . . included in the teaching of the eternal election of God to adoption and to eternal salvation." In my years of teaching the Lutheran heritage, I have come to expect a mild shock of surprise from students who learn for the first time that Lutherans, and not only Calvinists, hold to a doctrine of election. Then they are relieved to find out that it is not quite the same kind. Still, it is a difficult teaching. It smacks of philosophical or psychological determinism. One student said, "If I believed in it, I wouldn't be at the seminary." It seems to destroy freedom as the basic condition of meaning in history.

Election is the depth dimension in the certainty of faith that salvation proceeds from the grace of God alone and does not emerge from below as an element of our human potential. The content of election is the whole plan of God for the world. God not only foresees the salvation of humanity but sees to it. He brings to pass all that is needed, for which we are to thank, praise, and serve him. This means that we remain silent where Calvinists speak of "the horrible decrees of God." For election is framed by God's dealings with Israel and above all by his wonderful word of acceptance in Jesus Christ.

Something went wrong, however, in the Lutheran doctrine of election so that it no longer had the resonant ring of the gospel. What we see as wrong was never right in the first place; even Israel was able to pervert her election by grace into a religious elitism. Lutheran theologians began to query, "If all salvation is of grace, why are some saved and others not?" This is like asking: "Why are *we* saved instead of *them*?" Those who asked the question always assumed they were in the circle of the saved and showed little concern for the circle of the damned in the unmissionary era of Lutheran orthodoxy.

The confessions do not speculate on the doctrine of election. For the most part election is interpreted as an article of consolation to those who doubt in the throes of contingent human experiences. No matter what the to's and fro's of our subjective experience (consider Luther's *Anfechtungen*), God's grace is sure to see us through. God's grace does not waver like our feelings. Election has existential significance and is not a spurious piece of speculative metaphysics. It definitely prevents us from grounding our hope for the future in the human potential or the movement that goes by that name. The counsel to trust in yourself and let your own potential fly leads to existential despair and self-defeating humanism.

SOLA GRATIA AS A CRITIQUE OF RELIGION

In the twentieth century, Karl Barth recaptured the triumphant meaning of the Reformation *"sola gratia."*[7] He rightly taught us to differentiate between revelation and religion. Christianity, he said, is the religion of revelation, not the revelation of religion—obviously intending to attack the main trends of nineteenth-century Protestant theology. Revelation signifies an unveiling of God's otherwise hidden activity in the world; religion is our human response to what we take to be our God. Karl Barth created great offense, like the prophets of Israel, making clear that we are saved by grace alone, by God's self-revealing action, and not by our religious upward striving. *Sola gratia* is a prophetic critique of religion. And it needs to be renewed in our time.

Anders Nygren reinforced Barth's prophetic criticism of religion in his popular book, *Agapé and Eros.*[8] When the New Testament speaks of God's love for us, it uses the term *agapé*. When the Greek philosophers spoke of our human love for God, they used the term *eros*. Nygren pointed out that this distinction can help us understand what Christian faith means by the free grace of God. God's grace is an agapeic type of love—"spontaneous" and "unmotivated." God loves us because of his own free inner inclination to do so. There is no lovey-dovey quality within us that drives God to love us. God loves the unloveable, even the ungodly, "publicans and sinners," the enemies of public religion and morality.

God's love is furthermore "indifferent to value." His love shows no partiality to the righteous and pious people. He does not love us on account of any worthiness or righteousness within us. The most insidious temptation to the religious person is to believe that God will love me more if only I become more spiritual, and that divine blessings are granted or withheld in proportion to my performance, good or bad. The biblical concept of grace as agapeic love is calculated to attack every such notion of a bartering God and a bargain-counter religion.

If we say that God loves us irrespective of our inherent value, this does not mean that we have no value. Many of Nygren's critics mistakenly accused him of devaluing the creation, of denigrating the human—in short, of reviving the ancient Manichaean heresy. The same charge, of course, was mistakenly made against Luther's theology by the Council of Trent. What we mean to say is that we are infinitely precious and valuable in the sight of God because of his love. Only God's love places every human life beyond negotiation. Otherwise, life is precariously held in the balance of human calculation, judged from the point of view of *nomos* or *eros*. Christian respect for the infinite value of human life is grounded on the infinite love of God expressed in Jesus Christ. We are to love others even as God has loved us. God's love to us creates in us the capacity to love him in return and to love our fellow human beings with a selfless, self-spending, sacrificial love. Then we can even *love* those we do not *like*, because liking someone always depends on some likeable qualities of the person. We are commanded to *love* our enemies, not to *like* them. Not even God can make us do that.

Herein lies the essential difference between *agapé* and *eros*: *eros*-love is motivated by the value, beauty, and loveliness in the object of our liking. This type of love may be naturally directed to God who is absolutely identical with the good, the true, and the beautiful; or this *eros*-love may be expressed to a fellow human being in a romantic or sexual way. The latter is the usual sense in which we speak about erotic love. It would be more appropriate to speak of sexual love as libidinous love, to use Freud's term. The libido is the psychic drive to fulfill one's sexual instincts or one's instincts for pleasure. It is obvious that there is a vast difference between a pure *eros*-love for God who is inherently worthy of our love and a libidinous love on a sexual level. But there is also this similarity: in both cases we seek to fulfill deep longings and appetites within us, either of a spiritual or sexual kind.

But to say that we ought to express a pure love to God because God is good, true, and beautiful does not mean we can actually do so. Is this not the basic problem of human existence? We cannot do what we ought. We cannot elevate ourselves to the level of God in a relation of pure mutual love. We are creatures driven by fears, hostilities, and superstitions. Our heart, as Calvin said, is a "manufacturer of idols." We create gods we can control, and in worshiping them we are secretly worshiping ourselves. While professing to love God, we are actually loving a god-substitute created in our own image. Our natural human love to God becomes a perverted form of self-love. But even this we cannot do. We cannot even truly love ourselves. One perversion follows another. We hate ourselves in our very egocentricity. "Love God?" Luther cried. "I hate him!"

The cross of Christ as the power of God unto salvation declares that salvation is totally a work of God from beginning to end. The religions make it their business to atone for sin and guilt and to satisfy the demands of an angry God by evading God's judgment on all their works and ways in the cross of Christ. For this reason St. Paul could say that the cross is a religious scandal because it puts an end to salvation through religion and conveys salvation by the free gift of grace alone. This was the battle cry of the Reformation, and it is the touchstone of every gospel proclamation based on scriptural revelation. The word "alone" is essential to a theology of grace in order to grasp in a radical way the sovereignty of God's rule, the depth of human sinfulness, and the uniqueness of Jesus as Lord and Savior.

THE LADDERS TO HEAVEN

There are some ladders to heaven in the history of religion which people continually climb to ascend to God. They are "Towers of Babel" that must come down to drive people back to earth, to find God there at the utterly human level where he meets the world as a human being. The essential sin in the Tower of Babel story is that people are proudly storming the gates of heaven by their own strategy, skills, and strivings. They may be religious zealots, hoping to have fellowship with God on an equal level with God. The story of Adam and Eve is the story of our fall into sin, and sin consists in wanting to be as God. We do not by nature—our fallen nature—wish to accept God in the humble place where he has graciously chosen to disclose himself. We would expect to find God in a sacred temple or royal castle, not in a barn or on a cross. Our religious expectations are frustrated and reversed by the gospel.

There are three common attempts to build ladders or towers that reach to heaven.[9] These ladders can be found also in the church as it falls from the gospel back into the heavy stuff of religion. In the church the ladders are more dangerous than elsewhere because they are always embellished with a veneer of spirituality, moral zeal, and doctrinal rigor. The reformation of the church from the standpoint of justifying grace is never finished.

The first is the ladder of intellectualism. The intellectualist in religion is proud of the knowledge which can be acquired by the exercise of intellectual faculties. Intellectualism holds that the primary human faculty is reason, that humans are basically rational creatures. Therefore, one's relation to God is determined by one's knowledge of divine things. Salvation for this person comes by believing in doctrines which are either self-evidently rational or are certified by an authority whose rationality has been presumably demonstrated. We commonly hear some well-meant but distorted appeals to believe in certain doctrines to be saved. This enthusiasm for belief in Christian doctrines may become a distortion of faith in grace alone, for people may place their trust in the intellectual acceptance of true doctrinal ideas. Then salvation comes by believing assent to a system of thought rather than through faith in the gracious love of God in Jesus Christ.

People may trust in ideas as such rather than in the divine revelation symbolized and mediated by the ideas. The doctrines, of course, have their essential place in Christianity, but the intellectualist is more in love with the formulation of correct ideas than that to which the ideas point. The intellectualist easily becomes the dogmatist who fanatically asserts that to be saved everyone must hold the same correct ideas. Such a person grasps for earthly authorities to enforce conformity to a system of thought. The authority may be the Bible, the church, ecclesiastical creeds, or the Roman pope; then a relative authority within the Christian community is elevated to a position of absolute authority. The result is both blasphemy and idolatry, for only God possesses absolute authority.

God has not relinquished his absolute authority to any earthly subordinate, not even to the church or the Bible. We must come to despair of
our intellectual acumen *in loco justificationis*, realizing that not even our
finest intellectual endeavors can pile up credits toward our salvation. We
are not saved by the works of our intellect, not even if those works deal
with church doctrines or theological ideas. We are not saved by the theology we hold, not even if that theology is orthodox and confessionally
Lutheran.

Moralism is a second ladder; it is a matter of pride in ethical virtues
and loyalty to duty. It holds that the primary human faculty is the will,
that a person is basically a moral creature. Our relationship to God is
construed in legal categories as obedience to divine commandments. We
live then under the illusion that we are capable of obeying every "thou
shalt" uttered by God. We believe that God would not give a commandment unless we were able to fulfill the commandment by our own
willpower. We conceive of God as a celestial bookkeeper who keeps an
account of all the good and evil we do, reckoning with us on a debit and
credit basis. We must show a balance of merits to our credit in order to
gain salvation. The Christian moralist sees Jesus as a second Moses who
came to give humanity a new law. At best Jesus might be conceived as a
powerful inspiration to keep the law of God. Jesus for the moralist is
captured in legal categories, and these obstruct any encounter with Jesus
Christ in the grace categories of the New Testament.

The moralistic ladder to heaven must be smashed in order that we
might accept God's grace through faith alone apart from the works of the
law. The moralist is striving for righteousness, but the righteous person
cannot enter the kingdom of heaven. "They that be whole need not a
physician, but they that are sick." Harlots and derelicts are said to be
closer to the kingdom of grace, for they can provide no competition for
the righteousness of God in Jesus Christ. The moralist stands erect before
God praying, "God, I thank thee that I am not like those sinful people."
Jesus came into open conflict with the moralists of his day; they trusted
in themselves. Comparatively speaking, the Pharisees were righteous
people, but their righteousness was no help. It was a hindrance. The
gospel of grace in the story of Jesus convinces us that there are no human
works, not even the most eminent religious or moral works, in virtue of
which we can merit salvation. "For there is no distinction; since all have
sinned and fall short of the glory of God" (Rom. 3:22b-23).

Emotionalism in religion is a third ladder; it is apt to prescribe a certain
type of religious experience as the necessary condition for fellowship

with God. The religious faculty is assigned to the sphere of feeling. Religious worship becomes an occasion for *feeling* God's presence. The emotions are brought into play through stimulating sounds, rhythmic beats, or psychological gimmicks. The evangelist makes a big pitch for a person's decision while under the spell of excited feelings. The followers of feeling prefer that a person be able to relate a story in which the time and place of conversion can be pinpointed. The emotionalists have been largely Christians of the Third Article. They believe that somehow the Holy Spirit and feeling are coordinates, that the Holy Spirit is working to effect a certain emotional response.

There is no doubt that a human being is a creature of feeling and that feelings will be involved in the worship of God as much as anywhere. The danger in religious emotionalism is that people are lured into a false reliance upon their emotions. Emotions are the least dependable aspects of human experience. Reliance upon feelings in religion does not provide adequate resources in a crisis situation. No special quality of experience is required of us. Various emotional temperaments have been created by God; various kinds of emotional responses are to be expected. God does not prefer one specially enthusiastic kind. The charismatic movement is exploiting the emotional element in religious experience.

The total person combines the various dimensions of intellect, will, and feeling. If the whole person is being saved by the grace of God, every faculty of human experience will be involved in the redemptive process. Christian belief in the justifying grace of God *alone* is only concerned to insist that grace does not depend upon either intellectual, volitional, or emotional experiences. Rather, the creative grace of God redeems and sanctifies these dimensions of human experience and empowers them to magnify Christ unto the glory of God. Justification is an absolutely free gift of God's loving grace. This affirmation requires that we negate all trust in every possible ladder which people construct to gain salvation.

One more emphasis is needed to conclude this essay on justifying grace. We have reference to what we usually call the "means of grace." Between the grace of God revealed in the story of Jesus Christ of the first century and us moderns who live in the twentieth century, there is a chronological distance of nearly twenty centuries. How does a person today gain access to the gracious love of God manifest in Jesus Christ? Here is where heated differences arise between denominations. Lutheranism has steered a middle course between Protestantism, on the one hand, which places the Word alone at the center of Christianity and relegates the sacraments to the circumference and Roman Catholicism, on the other hand, which places the sacraments at the center and relegates the Word to the circumference. Each of these two emphases presents an abridged Christianity. Lutherans have stood confessionally for a full-bodied emphasis upon the Word *and* the Sacraments. The individual Christian and the whole church need to receive the forgiving grace of Christ and the renewal of life through the means which God has appointed for that purpose. We believe that the Scriptures, the witness and practice of the universal church in history, and the experience of the individual Christian overwhelmingly confirm the wisdom of stressing both the Word *and* the sacraments, neither one to the exclusion or suppression of the other.

By God's grace and the means of grace we can live meaningfully in time and history. We cannot realize our potentialities on our own. When the grace of God penetrates our life, we are equipped to deal with the three dimensions of time. We become free from bondage to our past through forgiveness; otherwise we are incarcerated in the guilts and fears which our past throws up to haunt us. We become fully engaged in the meaning of the present moment, living life to the hilt; otherwise we wander aimlessly through life, not knowing the whence and the whither of our movements. We are made open to the future which is rushing toward us, entering into the unknown with courage and faith in the providential hand of God; otherwise we are paralyzed into inaction, frozen by the foreboding possibilities of an incalculable tomorrow. Grace lifts us beyond bondage to the passage of time and mediates to us the power of eternal life.

NOTES

1. Martin Chemnitz, *Examination of the Council of Trent*, Part I, ed. Fred Kramer (St. Louis: Concordia Publishing House, 1971).

2. Ibid., p. 467.

3. Gustavo Gutierrez, *A Theology of Liberation*, trans. Sister Caridad Inda and John Eagleson (Maryknoll, N.Y.: Orbis Books, 1973), pp. 263-65.

4. Martin Chemnitz, *Examination of the Council of Trent*, p. 518.

5. Quoted by Anna Kähler, *Theologe und Christ: Erinnerungen und Bekenntnisse von Martin Kähler* (Berlin: Furche-Verlag, 1926). August Tholuck was Martin Kähler's teacher at the University of Halle.

6. Quoted by Karl Barth, *Church Dogmatics*, Vol. 4, pt. 1 (Edinburgh: T. & T. Clark, 1956), p. 617.

7. See G. C. Berkouwer's *The Triumph of Grace in the Theology of Karl Barth* (Grand Rapids, Mich.: Wm. B. Eerdmans, 1956).

8. Anders Nygren, *Agapé and Eros*, trans. Philip S. Watson (Philadelphia: Westminster Press, 1938).

9. Paul Tillich in *Dynamics of Faith* (New York: Harper & Brothers, 1957) writes about three distortions of faith, corresponding to these three "ladders to heaven." The three are the intellectualistic, the voluntaristic, and the emotionalistic distortions of the meaning of faith (Chapter 2).

7   The Two-Kingdoms Principle

THE THEOLOGICAL PROBLEM OF HUMAN RIGHTS

Jürgen Moltmann has laid down a challenge to the churches to work toward a truly ecumenical theology of human rights.[1] There are theological differences in the understanding of the theological basis of human rights between our Lutheran tradition and the Catholic and Reformed traditions. The fact that we lack common ground on this issue is a theoretical problem fraught with serious practical consequences. In February 1980, the National Council of Churches adopted a policy statement bearing on human rights with a four-page theological basis. The Lutheran Church in America (LCA) opposed the statement on the ground that this theological statement was not sufficiently ecumenical. In fact, the Lutherans said, the theological section was exclusively Reformed or Calvinistic and therefore not one that transcends our particular traditions in an ecumenical way.

The lack of a clear theological basis of human rights is not only a problem between our traditions but also within them. On a trip to Chile in 1975, I arrived in Santiago two days after a dramatic split between two factions within the Evangelical Church in Chile. The one faction led by Bishop Helmut Frenz and the majority of the pastors took sides in defending human rights. The other, led by powerful laity, appealed to Article XXVIII of the Augsburg Confession as backing for the traditional two-kingdoms doctrine, which allegedly calls for pastors to preach the gospel and leave politics to the government. Instead, the bishop and his pastors were protesting actions of the government in violation of human rights, helping to resettle political refugees, and ministering to relatives of disappearing persons. They were supposedly guilty of confusing the two kingdoms, thus mixing the church's message with the issue of human rights.

The problem for Lutherans is not of recent vintage. In the nineteenth century there developed within Lutheranism a rigid dualism of two separate spheres, one having to do with this earthly life, politics and all, the other with eternal life, everything pertaining to salvation. The Lutheran dogmatician, Christian Luthardt, for example, wrote: "The Gospel has absolutely nothing to do with outward existence but only with eternal life . . . It is not the vocation of Jesus Christ or of the Gospel to change the orders of secular life and establish them anew . . . Christianity wants to change man's heart, not his external situation."[2] Similarly, Rudolf Sohm wrote that the issues of public life "should remain untouched by the proclamation of the Gospel, completely untouched."[3] This dualistic scheme was enormously influential also upon the Lutheran immigrant theology in the United States, accounting for the characteristically Lutheran habit of thinking in two realms, putting the Word and the sacraments into one, public life and human rights into the other.

The result of such dichotomizing of life into two spheres, public and private, proved fateful in the twentieth century. There is a certain dualistic interpretation of the two kingdoms which completely paralyzes the nerve of the church on the issues of justice and human rights. What do human rights have to do with a gospel that relates only to the inner life of faith and the afterlife of hope? Is it too strong to speak of this monstrous distortion of Luther's teaching on the two kingdoms as a "Lutheran heresy," constituting as serious a threat to the integrity of the gospel in modern times as Gnosticism or Arianism in the ancient church? Lutheran champions of the two-kingdoms doctrine advanced the thesis, after Hitler's rise to power, that "there is no contradiction between an unconditional allegiance to the Gospel, on the one hand, and a similarly unconditional allegiance to the German national, that is, to the National-Socialist state, on the other."[4] Karl Barth objected in a counter-thesis, stating that anyone who speaks of two unconditional allegiances places himself outside the Evangelical Church.[5] That person is, in short, a heretic.

This is not at all a problem confined to German Lutheranism. The same defect has been operative among Lutherans in current history—in Chile, South Africa, and North America. For example, the Lutheran leadership was silent during America's war in Vietnam. There was fear of bringing the external war home to the congregations. The operative assumption was clear: the church's business is to preach the gospel, administer the sacraments, and care for souls in anguish; the government is in charge of the nation's life, foreign policy, and civil rights. The words of one well-known Lutheran theologian could be quoted:

> Every man is a member of a secular realm and of a spiritual realm. It is important to realize the difference between these two realms and to keep them separate. Luther claimed that Jesus (Matt. 22:21) had emphasized the separation of the two realms when he said: 'Render therefore unto Caesar the things which are Caesar's, and unto God the things that are God's.' Luther himself pointed frequently to the difference between the two and reiterated the need for a clear separation.[6]

These words are susceptible to ideological misappropriation. Who could expect this type of doctrine to motivate Christians to move to the frontline in the struggle for peace and justice, for the human rights of all people?

The story of theology's entanglement with the violation of basic human rights does not end with the Lutheran two-kingdoms doctrine. The most notorious denial of human rights is taking place in South Africa under the aegis of the Afrikaners' redaction of Calvinist exodus-theology. The God of the covenant is engaged in repeating his adventures with biblical Israel, only now the elect are not Jews but Calvinists. The history of Israel is recapitulated in the Afrikaners' struggle for freedom from their British oppressors. The South African sociologist, T. Dunbar Moodie, has stressed the underlying theological character of his country's history: "The divine agent of the Afrikan civil faith is Christian and Calvinist—an active sovereign God who calls the elect, who promises and punishes, who brings forth life from death in the course of history."[7] Apartheid is seemingly justifiable as policy if one can claim Israel's subduing of Canaan as the anticipation of the trekkers' journey to a new land of promise peopled by heathen. Here we have quite the opposite of the two-kingdoms doctrine, a biblicist covenant theology with a koinonia-ethic, providing no basis for universal human rights, that is, the rights of Canaanites on a par with Jews, the rights of heathen on a par with Christians.

If we look to Latin America we can find numerous examples of human rights violations in a dominantly Roman Catholic context. Liberation theology is currently challenging the traditional nature/grace scheme which has provided the ideological undergirding for the kind of partnership the church has enjoyed with the ruling minorities.

These are but a few samples of how our particular theological traditions—Lutheran, Reformed, and Roman Catholic—have been steeped in social systems which exhibit glaring insensitivity to universal human rights. Our aim in this chapter is to set forth the theological foundations of human rights with an ecumenical bias, aiming not simply to repristinate but to transcend the limits of each tradition and to find common ground. Thus, we are dealing with the *theological* problem of human rights.

THE ECUMENICAL TRIANGLE

We will start our discussion of the theological foundations of human rights with a comparison of the different approaches of the Reformed, Lutheran, and Roman Catholic traditions. Jürgen Moltmann states that the Reformed approach grounds human rights in the *imago dei* as witnessed within the covenant community, in line with the tradition of federal theology. The disadvantage in the Reformed position is that by presupposing the community of faith, it is acceptable only to Christians. But this weak point is at the same time its strong point, for in speaking to Christians it can motivate and activate them to a concern for human rights.

Moltmann points to recent Lutheran World Federation publications on human rights as the basis for his characterization of the two-kingdoms teaching. In this view human rights are secular phenomena which Christians share with all others on the basis of their common humanity. There is no specifically Christian foundation of human rights; reason not faith provides the mode of access to the basis and contents of human rights. However, these recent Lutheran efforts (Moltmann cites Tödt and Huber, in particular) are obviously striving to overcome a pure dichotomy of Christian faith and human rights, so they recognize in human rights "similarities and analogies" to the Christian faith. Although they remain secular, human rights point beyond themselves to the promises of the gospel. Moltmann concludes by observing some convergence between the Reformed and the Lutheran conceptions. The Reformed view starts *from above*, from God's claim on humanity, as well as *from within*, from inside the covenant community, and proceeds to ground the rights of all human beings on this specifically Christian theological basis, whether non-Christians can share these perspectives or not. The Lutheran view starts *from below*, from our common human experience, as well as *from outside*, beyond the theological circle in the secular realm, and proceeds to find correspondences between the concrete elements of human rights and the basic contents of Christian faith. The question remains open, therefore, how best to relate the particularity of Christian faith to the universality of human rights.

Moltmann finds that the official statements of the Roman Catholic Church still use the Thomistic schema of nature and grace. Our knowl edge of human rights is based on natural law. Reason is capable of grasping and defining the basic rights that inhere in universal human nature. The natural law theory can easily lay claim to a universal horizon. Grace enters in as a supplement to nature, as the fulfilling destiny of humankind in light of the gospel. *Gratia non tollit sed perficit naturam.* This view grounds the universalism of human rights in nature, reason, justice, and law common to all people. The fact that over a hundred nations can subscribe to the United Nations' Universal Declaration of Human Rights without any reference to the Bible, Christ, or the gospel would seem to support the Roman Catholic notion of a natural law universally present in humankind.

This is as far as Moltmann's reflections on the "ecumenical triangle" take us, registering important theological differences and still open questions.

THE NATURE OF LAW

All three traditions must appeal to law in the common human task of formulating and realizing human rights, no matter how different their starting points, whether law before gospel (the Lutheran view), or covenant before law (the Reformed view), or natural law before supernatural grace (the Roman Catholic view). All three face the same secularized culture in which both the theory and rule of law are in deep crisis. The rise of the positivistic theory of law prepared the way for the abuse of law by the totalitarian state, manipulating it as a mere function of absolute power.[8] Prior to the triumph of positivism, the law was thought to be a means of justice administered by the state, not a tool of arbitrary power. With the collapse of theological and/or metaphysical foundations of justice, there was no other base of support, no other source, no other criterion of validity for the law than the will of those who held the monopoly of force.

The twentieth century has witnessed with unforgettable horror the "lawlessness of law." Legal positivism stands defenseless, stripped of the traditional appeal to transcendent norms of justice beyond positive law. Positivism cannot go beyond the question "What does the law say?" to the question "What *ought* the law to say?" In positivistic theory, justice is determined by what the law says, not the law by what justice requires. Such a doctrine makes judges the captive flunkies of the government in power. The atrocities committed by the state against its citizens can therefore be legalized, for the law becomes the slave of the state, not a servant of justice to which the authority of the state itself is subordinate.

The fear of normlessness and its nihilistic effects in the field of human rights has sparked a revival of interest in the classical notion of natural law.[9] Churches also have been shocked into a renewed sense of responsibility for the process of law in social life. Yet with all the conferences held and position papers written, there has emerged no consensus on the theological foundation of law. Many questions remain unsettled. What is the proper theological response to legal positivism? Are Christian ethics and natural law antithetical or complementary? Is there a Christian natural law? Is the Christian interpretation of law to be based on the First Article of the Apostles' Creed, as in the Erlangen theology of the orders of creation (and also by Wingren in Sweden)? Or is it to be derived from Christology, as Karl Barth proposed? Or is there another way of understanding the source and function of law which both overcomes the most serious limitations in the Catholic natural law theory, in the Lutheran doctrine of the orders of creation, or in the Barthian christological ethics, and yet hopes to retain the deepest elements of truth and relevance in each? We would not wish to accomplish less than a comprehensive synthesis in an ecumenical theology of human rights. A complete repudiation of any one of the three approaches seems impossible to me. First of all, they are not mutually exclusive alternatives in every respect; second, each has developed in its own way in response to a particular historical situation; and third, each one calls attention to some deficiency in the others.

Both the Roman Catholic and Lutheran traditions hold to the priority of law as a universally given structure of common human experience. The perennial appeal of the idea of natural law can be explained by its reference to a universal justice and moral law to which all persons have access through their reason and conscience. Natural law proclaims clear and unambiguous moral principles rooted in a universal human nature. However, it fell upon hard times with the dawn of the age of historical consciousness. Skepticism arose over against the notion of an immutable order of moral standards which transcend the relativities of time and space. Legal positivism was the logical outcome of historical relativism. Natural law, along with natural theology, was subjected to severe theological criticism. Protestant theologians, encouraged by Karl Barth, pointed out that natural law shared in a non-biblical view of a static world, presupposed a deistic view of the relation between God and the creation, and did not take seriously the consequences of sin upon human reason and will. Moreover, Christian theology inherited natural law theory from the Greek and Roman philosophers, befitting a metaphysical picture of the world as nature rather than the biblical picture of the world as history.

Are there really universal laws of nature inscribed into the granite-like structure of things? If so, it is hard to see how they can mesh gears with the dynamics of history as a realm of intentions, free decisions, novel situations, and unique events. A new-style natural law will have to emerge under the new conditions of historical understanding and in light of the biblical eschatological horizon of the kingdom of God, if it is to satisfy the demands of modernity and Christian faith. This proposal to shift from the statics of traditional metaphysics to the dynamics of history opening toward the eschatological future of God can carry us beyond our denominational particularisms toward a common ecumenical frame of reference.

The Lutheran theology of the orders of creation[10] was an attempt to overcome the latent deism in natural law theory by deriving law from the doctrine of God the Creator, hence, not *lex naturae* but *lex creationis!* At the same time, this Lutheran theology shared the interest of natural law to find a common basis on which Christians and non-Christians alike could cooperate in the realization of human rights. Such a basis would be independent of uniquely Christian convictions which derive from the special revelation of God in Jesus Christ. Human beings exist within certain orders of creation such as marriage, family, state, and the like. However, just as natural law theory was criticized for its unhistorical character, so also the idea of the orders of creation became subjected to the same criticism. Hence, Wolfhart Pannenberg could raise this question: "Are there really orders which uniformly underlie all social forms that have arisen in history and of which the historical forms are only variations? Does not every social form bear through and through the mark of history?"[11] Historical research and cultural anthropology help us to see more readily how theology has frequently succumbed to the temptation to provide absolute ideological justification for quite transient formations of life. A certain fluidity entered in when some Lutheran theologians made a distinction between orders of creation and orders of preservation. This issue bears on the matter of human rights because such things as class and race have sometimes been traced back to the orders of creation and would thus presumably bear the imprint of the Creator's original design. At times Christian theology has been behind in affirming universal human rights because it has identified certain historical forms with the eternal will of God. Many church leaders obstructed the democratic revolutions of modern times on the ground of the divine right of kings.

Karl Barth was right to criticize the Lutheran notion of the "orders of creation" as an autonomous locus of theology completely *separate* from the revelation of God in Jesus Christ. Our Christian understanding of justice must be related to the gospel of justification.[12] The lack of a christological center and criterion in the theology of the orders of creation became the legitimate point of departure for the Barthian attack on the Lutheran social ethic.

The chief concern of Karl Barth is the confession of the universal lordship of Christ. Barth's claim is that not only the church but also the state stands under the lordship of Christ. This sounds like an unobjectionable formula of faith. But what is the practical meaning of affirming the lordship of Christ in the realm of government, law, industry, labor relations, sport, and every sphere in which human rights are at stake? Barth is so intent on overcoming the hidden "natural theology" in the German Lutheran doctrine of the state that he somehow derives the state directly from Christology. What becomes most problematic is his use of the principle of analogy to derive concrete norms from the circle of the Christian community to apply to the civil community.[13] This approach, however, fails to account for the fact that the international consensus on human rights exists without any epistemic connection with the confession of Christ. Theology may hold to a hidden connection between Christology and human rights in the order of being (*ordo essendi*) but not so directly in the order of knowledge (*ordo cognoscendi*). Indirectly, it may be argued, the present consensus on human rights has been achieved to a great extent through the historical mediation of the Christian consciousness, although in the West all traces of this historical connection with the Christian faith have been erased by the impact of the Enlightenment and the process of secularization.

The Lutheran concern has been for a clear differentiation between law and gospel as two modes of divine activity in the world. The two-kingdoms doctrine is an expression of this distinction. This means that human rights can be defined and realized in common among Christians and non-Christians without reference to the gospel as the condition of this possibility. The Barthian concern is for the ultimate unity of gospel and law under the one Lord so that no sphere of existence can remain outside his dominion and no rival to his rule can be acknowledged by the Christian. These two dimensions of concern are not incompatible. In the light of the revelation of God in Jesus Christ, Christians possess a new basis for *understanding* the realities of government and law. However, these realities are established by God prior to the incarnation of Jesus Christ and can at least be partially understood and administered by those who do not acknowledge the lordship of Christ. Such a thesis can be maintained if it can be shown that the political activity of the living God in the world is not limited by our *knowledge* of the historical revelation in Jesus Christ. God reveals himself through creation and law. This does not mean that Christology is once again removed from the center. In the New Testament there is a "cosmic Christology" which expresses that the Christ who is Jesus in the flesh is also the medium of creation and the fulfillment of the law. Christology cannot be confined to the ghetto of soteriology. Therefore, also, the meaning of the law must be interpreted from a christological perspective, but not in such a way that Christians would claim to be able to derive specific social principles from Christology. There is no specifically Christian "bill of rights."

THE FUNCTION OF LAW

We have argued that the law is the common denominator for an ecumenical theology of human rights. This means that although law and gospel are closely connected, human knowledge of the contents of the law is not dependent on belief in the gospel. This must be so in the order of knowledge, whether with the Lutherans we prefer the formula "law before gospel" or with the Barthians "gospel before law." Everything depends on our angle of inquiry. If we confine our attention to the sequence of events in the covenant history of the Bible, then it is possible to argue that Yahweh's election of Israel happened before the giving of the law for the ordering of the community's life. Thus, gospel promise precedes covenant law. On the other hand, Israel herself wrote a preamble (Genesis 1–11) to her own covenant history, involving the whole human race, placing Adam before Abraham and Noah before Moses. The living God was at work among the nations of the world prior to the election of Israel, and God acts in the realm of international relations today without any direct contact with the preaching of his Word. The instrument of his activity is the law, and this law confronts every person, community, and nation in his, her, or its actual empirical existence, creating a degree of order in spite of the destructive consequences of sin.

The knowledge of God is not the presupposition for the acknowledgment of basic human rights and needs. Atheists and agnostics and humanists know the *law* of God without faith in the *God* of law. Christians confess that God is active through the law that is operative in the world, whether people confess the name of God or not. The order of divine activity does not correspond to the order of human knowledge. God carries out his political purposes through political leaders and institutions whether they know it or not. There is no sphere of life where God is not active through the law to secure and advance the basic dignity of human beings. God works through the law of human existence, that is, through the essential structure of humanity (the *imago dei*) which is struggling to become actual in concrete life. This rule of law through the actual demands given in concrete existence is not to be equated with the laws we find in the Bible. Christian theology has rightly seen that the second table of the decalogue summarizes a rudimentary knowledge of law that is universally valid in human life and can be known apart from biblical history and revelation. The fact that such a summary is possible indicates that there is a constant element in the history of God's activity in human society and in the relations which people enjoy in human community. Natural law theory holds that there are certain constants within the variables, but it accounts for this through an abstract doctrine of human nature and reason rather than as the continuing pressure of the living God through the concrete demands which impinge inescapably on all human beings. In Luther's language, this is the work of God's left hand.

If we see the law of God as a driving force behind the rights which human beings claim from each other, we should not equate the specific contents of these claims at any given time with an "eternal list of rights" in the mind of God above and beyond history. The question arises: What is the criterion of the just demands of the law at any given time? What is right? The answer is: We possess the critical standpoint in the ideal of justice. But how can the ideal of justice act as a means of testing what is constitutive of human rights? The core of justice is care for the neighbor. Justice is the form that love takes in the life of society. The sum of the law is: You are to love your neighbor as yourself. If you love your neighbor, you will care for him/her, which means that you will concern yourself with his/her basic rights.

In traditional language, the political or civil use of the law places demands on me to serve my neighbor in need, whether I feel like it or not. There is no escape from the law; everywhere I go I meet neighbors whose rights I must acknowledge in some way. Law functions as pressure on me to do what is beneficial to my neighbor, without regard for my feelings toward that person. The law is universal because it requires all citizens to give others their due and threatens punishment if they do not.

The superior way to meet the demands of the neighbor and to acknowledge his/her rights is out of the pure motivation of love for that person. But love is not the universal motive behind the social demand to grant the human rights of all people. The force of law and the threat of punishment make people respond out of fear. Law is the common ground of human rights in a world of sin.

THE TWO-KINGDOMS PERSPECTIVE

In an ecumenical age Lutheran theology must be sensitive about the way in which it constructs an apologia for its traditional two-kingdoms perspective. Does the two-kingdoms teaching provide an adequate framework for making the proper distinction between law and gospel, justice and love, government and grace, the rights of humans realized on earth and the righteousness of God revealed from heaven? What is the irreducible minimum of truth in the two-kingdoms doctrine? Recent Luther research has freed Lutherans to be critical of the common assumption that their two-kingdoms doctrine can be simply traced back to Luther himself. Luther, of course, never wrote a systematic treatise on "the doctrine of the two kingdoms." However, the elements of a complex and highly differentiated doctrine of the two kingdoms can be found in all of Luther's sermons and writings. What is non-negotiable in this teaching? It can only be that which belongs to the essence of the gospel itself, not some chauvinistic loyalty that forces Lutherans to swallow the husks of the sixteenth-century sociopolitical situation.

There are two kingdoms in conflict: the kingdom of God and the kingdom of Satan. Of course, a theology with no Satan (as Wingren says of Barth's theology) will have some trouble with this type of dualism. This is not a "God is in heaven and man is on earth" type of dualism, as Barth expressed it in his early period. The broad backdrop of the gospel picture of Jesus as the Christ features the power of God against the powers of evil at work in the whole of creation. Jesus brings the power of God's rule into history, confronts the demonic forces, and wins a victory which spells ultimate freedom for human beings.

This antithesis between God and Satan is one kind of dualism in Luther which cannot be surrendered without making nonsense of everything he said. But there is another of equal importance. This is the dualism between two contrasting modes of divine activity in and through the world. We cannot accept a reduction of the language of faith—which symbolizes God's relation to the world—to a single dimension. Luther spoke of "the two hands of God." The "left hand of God" is a formula meaning that God is universally at work in human life through structures and principles commonly operative in political, economic, and cultural institutions that affect the life of all. The struggle for human rights occurs within this realm of divine activity. However, no matter how much peace and justice and liberty are experienced in these common structures of life, they do not mediate "the one thing needful." This is the function of the gospel of God in Jesus Christ, the work of the "right hand of God." The scandal of the gospel is that salvation is a sheer gift of grace, given freely by God for Christ's sake and received through faith alone. It is meritorious for a society to grant and guarantee to all its citizens the basic human rights, but high marks in this area do not translate into the righteousness that counts before God in the absolute dimension.

It is essential to Christian faith to make the right distinctions between law and gospel and between the two kingdoms. The commingling of law and gospel as well as the confusion of the two modes of divine activity have disastrous consequences for theology and the church. But *distinction* does not mean *separation*. The two kingdoms are not spheres that can be separated but dimensions to be distinguished. There is no political sphere alongside a spiritual sphere. The two kingdoms must not be confused with the modern idea of the separation of church and state. The cosmic struggle between the divine and the satanic forces penetrates every dimension of human life, including the religious. The twofold involvement of God means that, on the one hand, he works creatively to promote what is good for human life in all its personal and social dimensions and, on the other hand, he works redemptively to bring the world forward to that final perfection summed up in Christ.

Lutherans should make clear that they are not hung up on the terminology of the two kingdoms or on Luther's language about the two hands of God. What we are after is only what belongs to the truth of the gospel, what is essential for Christian identity and the practice of the Christian faith. What belongs to the gospel belongs to the whole church. No theology can be ecumenical at all which is not grounded in just this gospel. "No other gospel" should not become a slogan of the conservative wing of the church, as though the liberals possessed some other basis of Christian faith. The Christian message in its totality, therefore, speaks of two things that God is doing in the world. God is pressing for the historical liberation of human beings through a host of secular media, and for Christ's sake he promises eternal salvation through the preaching of the Word and the administration of the sacraments. Historical liberation and eternal salvation are not one and the same thing. They should not be equated. The gospel is not one of the truths we hold to be self-evident; it is not an inalienable right which the best government in the world can do anything about. There are many people fighting valiantly on the front-line of legitimate liberation movements who are not in the least animated by the gospel. The hope for liberation is burning in the hearts of millions of little people struggling to free themselves from conditions of poverty and tyranny. When they win this freedom, should they be so fortunate, they have not automatically therewith gained the freedom for which Christ has set us free (Gal. 5:1.) This is the barest minimum of what we intend to convey by the two-kingdoms perspective.

THE ESCHATOLOGICAL HORIZON

The famous Chalcedonian formula speaks of the two natures of Christ in a way that we could appropriate for the two kingdoms: "without confusion, without change, without division, without separation."[14] But then we are faced with the analogous problem that vexed the post-Chalcedonian theologians: What is the principle of their unity? The search for the answer carried theologians into speculation about the hypostatic unity, *anhypostasia, enhypostasia,* the *communicatio idiomatum,* and the like. We have a similar problem. How shall we conceive the principle of unity that links the two dimensions of God's revelation through the law of creation and the gospel of redemption? Oddly, Lutherans have traditionally veered toward the Monophysitic side in their Christology but have tended to be "Nestorian" in their treatment of the two kingdoms.

The principle of unity we are looking for is available to us by reactivating the eschatological horizon of the Bible. The realm of creation and the realm of redemption share the same eschatological future horizon. The doctrines of creation and law are linked to the eschatological goal of the world to which the church points in its message of the coming kingdom. The theme of eschatology relates not only to the order of salvation (*ordo salutis*) but also to the fact and future of ongoing creation. The orders of creation are not autonomous; there is an eschatological consummation (*apokatastasis ton panton*) of all things previewed and preenacted in the life, death, and resurrection of Jesus the Christ of God. In the gospel picture of Jesus Christ we witness the unity of the struggle for human rights and the embodiment of divine righteousness. The struggles for rights waged by peasants, by the proletariat, and by the wretched of the earth are claimed by the gospel as the very ones in whose midst the signs of the messianic kingdom are to erupt. The Messiah comes, we are told, when "the blind see, the lame walk, lepers are cleansed, the deaf hear, the dead are raised up, and the poor are hearing good news."

The eschatological message of the Christian faith thus offers the churches today the potential for an ecumenically based theology of human rights. Human rights are not "secular," as though they had only to do with "law and order," with no bearing on Jesus' message of the kingdom. The values embodied in the international consensus on human rights and the efforts to realize them in social life can be interpreted as earthly signs of the justice of the kingdom of God which the gospel announces to the world on the basis of the justification which God has granted through Jesus Christ.

The church's eschatological message thus combines the two dimensions of hope: hope for the poor and hope for sinners. The poor clamor for justice and sinners cry for justification. It is intolerable for the church to separate these concerns. The church is to take the message of the kingdom into the real world where the demons are running riot and where the hand of God is stirring the cauldron of secular existence in all its political, economic, and social dimensions. We must strive for a comprehensive understanding of the kingdom of God which embraces two dimensions at the same time. The *vertical* dimension of the gospel mediates an encounter with the absolute transcendence of God; the *horizontal* dimension of the coming kingdom speaks of the encounter with Christ in the person of our needy neighbor. The *depth* dimension reveals our human condition of sin and estrangement; the *breadth* dimension tangles with the powers of evil on the plane of everyday historical existence. The *personal* dimension lifts up each individual as infinitely valuable in the sight of God; the *political* dimension looks to the quality of justice and liberty that prevails in the land. The symbol of the kingdom of God is multidimensional, uniting these vertical and personal dimensions with horizontal and political dimensions of the coming kingdom.

The question which faces the two-kingdoms type of dualism is whether the church and its missionary outreach can join in the creative task of bringing the vertical line of justification through faith alone to bear on the horizontal line of the kingdom striving for justice in an evil world. The upward line linking the transcendence of God to the personal experience of faith must intersect with the forward line where the struggles for human rights, peace, and freedom are joined. The upward line of faith is connected with the forward line of history in the story of their interplay in the ministry of Jesus the Christ. In other words, the upward line of salvation through Christ is tied to the forward line of liberation in

history. The love of God for Christ's sake and the commitment to human
rights for the sake of humanity are joined in the picture of what God is
doing for the world in the history of Jesus Christ. The one God involved
in the struggle for human liberation from hunger, misery, oppression, ignorance, and all the powers of sin and evil is none other than the Father
of Jesus Christ who is reconciling the whole world to himself. The signs
of liberation are anticipations of the total salvation the world is promised
in Christ.

The rule of God's righteousness revealed in the ministry of Jesus is the
total and final power of God to secure in the end the fulfillment of human
rights which are often denied and at best only partially realized under the
conditions of earthly existence. The power of eschatological righteousness is already now at work to put things right between human beings, to
make things right for people who do not stand in the right before God,
who do not do what is right, who in fact are guilty of violating the rights
of others in self-righteous aggression, and who rob God of his rights and
of his due by putting him down in their pride. A community blessed with
the knowledge of the gift of God's absolute righteousness in Christ will
have no other choice but to be the advocate of every dimension of earthly righteousness (*iustitia civilis*) that can be realized on earth.

There are many ways in which the church on this basis can and must
share in the universally human struggle for human rights. First of all, the
church is to preach the whole counsel of God, which includes the politics
of the kingdom of God through the means of justice and law (the *regnum
potentiae; the usus legis politicus*). Second, the church is to intercede for
the victims of oppression whose rights are being negated in any way, re-
membering them in prayer before God. Third, the church is to be a dem-
onstration before the world of how human beings might live together
fully respecting one another's rights, modeling possibilities of existence
available to all people. Fourth, the church will teach all its members to
practice the Christian life through their secular vocations in the world.
Fifth, the church is to be a vigilant and militant mission against the forces
at work to deprive people of their basic rights. Sixth, the church must do
the works of mercy, accepting responsibility to do whatever possible to
defend and rescue those whose rights are being trampled down by the
powers that be. Seventh, the church must establish in its schools centers
of research in order to pioneer social sensitivity to new forms of oppression and to put the spotlight of compassion on the invisible victims.

This is not an exhaustive statement, but it shows that the Christian
community cannot remain behind a phony wall of separation between

church and state, religion and society, law and gospel, the kingdom on
the left and the kingdom on the right hand of God, and so on. I have expressed my conviction that the direction in which to move to overcome
these separations for the sake of a genuine ecumenically and theologically grounded Christian understanding of human rights is provided by the
new affirmation of the kingdom of God as the starting point and organiz-
ing principle for systematic theology. Such an emphasis does not belong
to any one of the three traditions with which we have been dealing. We
all read the same Gospels. We are all challenged by the results of modern
biblical scholarship. These perspectives have the power to relativize the
exclusivistic tendencies and to open up a new horizon of common understanding beyond all of them.

NOTES

1. Jürgen Moltmann, "Christian Faith and Human Rights," *How Christian
Are Human Rights?* ed. Eckehart Lorenz (Geneva: Lutheran World Federation,
1981).
2. See Karl H. Hertz, ed., *Two Kingdoms and One World: A Sourcebook in
Christian Social Ethics* (Minneapolis: Augsburg Publishing House, 1976), p. 84.
3. Ibid., p. 87.
4. Quoted from "The Rengsdorf Theses" in Hertz, *Two Kingdoms and One
World*, p. 184.
5. Ibid., p. 185.
6. George W. Forell, "Luther's Conception of 'Natural Orders,'" *Lutheran
Church Quarterly* 18 (1945):166.
7. T. Dunbar Moodie, *The Rise of Afrikanerdom* (Berkeley, Calif.: University of California Press, 1975), p. ix.
8. For discussions on the origin, nature and consequences of legal positivism,
see the following: John C. Bennett, *Christians and the State* (New York: Charles
Scribner's Sons, 1958), Chap. 8, "The Law of the State and the State under Law";
Anders Nygren, "Christianity and Law," *Dialog* 1, 4 (Autumn 1962).
9. The vitality of this attempt to recover the notion of natural law is not
limited to Roman Catholic scholars. Cf. John Cogley, Robert M. Hutchins, et al.,
eds., *Natural Law and Modern Society* (Cleveland: World Publishing, 1962). See
also the report by Heinz-Horst Schrey, "Die Wiedergeburt des Naturrechts,"
Theologische Rundschau 19, 1, 2, 3.
10. For a classic statement of this theology, see Paul Althaus, *Theologie der
Ordnungen* (Gütersloh: Gütersloher Verlagshaus, 1935). See also Werner Elert,
The Christian Ethos, trans. Carl J. Schindler (Philadelphia: Muhlenberg Press,
1957).
11. Wolfhart Pannenberg, "Zur Theologie des Rechts," *Zeitschrift für
Evangelische Ethik* 7, 1 (January 1963): 3-4.
12. The most important writings of Karl Barth on this issue are: "Evangelium

und Gesetz," *Theologische Existenz Heute,* Heft 32 (München, 1935); "Rechtfertigung und Recht," *Theologische Studien,* Heft 1 (Zollikon-Zürich, 1938); "Christengemeinde und Bürgergemeinde," *Theologische Studien,* Heft 20 (Zollikon-Zürich, 1946).

13. Emil Brunner criticized Barth's application of the principle of analogy. He wrote, "Per analogiam, Barth now derives norms from the Christian Church for the civil community, but he evidently does not notice that anything and everything can be derived from the same principle of analogy: a monarchy just as much as a republic (Christ the King), the totalitarian state, just as much as a state with civil liberties (Christ the Lord of all; man a servant, indeed a slave of Jesus Christ.)" *The Christian Doctrine of Creation and Redemption* (Philadelphia: Westminster Press, 1952), p. 319.

14. The suggestion was advanced by Gustaf Aulén, "Gospel and law are closely united. In fact, we could here apply the famous Chalcedonian formula about the relations between the two natures of Christ: 'without confusion, without change, without division, without separation.'" *Church, Law, and Society* (New York: Charles Scribner's Sons, 1948), p. 57.

Indexes

INDEX OF NAMES

INDEX OF SUBJECTS